Kitchen Wisdom Gluten Free©

Author Liz Conforti

Journey into a Culinary Cultural Evolution

Learn How to Transform Southern Italian Recipes

To their Enticing Gluten Free Complement

Food & Recipe Blog kitchenwisdomglutenfree.com

Facebook   Pinterest   Twitter   Instagram   Tumblr   Google+

In Honor of Those Who Came Before Me

Acknowledgements

I have eternal gratitude and thanks. My honey, Kenny, thank you for your love, encouragement, support and your belief in me and this project - None of this would have been possible without you. Thanks mom for your love and support, experience, willingness to share and participate in this project with me. Thanks to my incredible friends: Chrisanne, Deb, Evelyn, Gino & Maureen, Gwen, Kira, Pete, Stacy, Thea, and Terri I am so appreciative for your love, encouragement and belief in me. I am so fortunate that all of the people I am closest to in the world have taken time from their lives to help me and this project in some way. Without everyone, the birthing of *Kitchen Wisdom Gluten Free* would not have been possible - thank you and countless blessings to you all!

About the Author

Liz Conforti, grew up with her hands in a well of flour, learning authentic recipes from her elders who immigrated to New York City from the Campania region surrounding Naples, Italy. She has spent ten years living gluten free and re-creating family recipes with gluten free ingredients.   Residing in Vermont, away from her childhood communities, she reaches out as an impressive food blogger intent on illuminating the enigma of delicious gluten free cooking and baking.

Table of Contents

Preface

Throughout this book there are conversations and recollections which reflect the wisdom of my elders. They spoke in *Kitchen Wisdom*, offering practical guidance on how to prepare foods and approach life. I have been re-creating, in gluten free, the recipes of my family - those particular baked and cooked dishes from the *Old Country* (the Province of Caserta in the Region of Campania in Italy - specifically the towns of Santa Maria A Vico & Calvanico). I call the experience *communing with My Ancestors*.

I was plagued for years with various medical symptoms that were chronic. Living without pain and discomfort associated with gluten is wonderful. I officially have NCGS (Non-Celiac Gluten Sensitivity), which is an immune system based response to an allergen. However, my symptoms are most likely Celiac Disease (CD). Like many others, it would be medically dangerous to re-introduce gluten into my diet for 3 months, so I can take the Celiac Disease test. Either way, I will live a lifelong diet without consumption and exposure to gluten. Living without the foods I was raised with, not so wonderful. Going gluten free is more than food change, it is a lifestyle change.

I realized, even though I knew to combine ingredients in wheat flour recipes, I really didn't understand the chemistry of baking. My elders taught me how to make the magic happen with gluten rich flours, but I never learned the chemistry of the magic. Anyone who grew up eating gluten rich foods and baked goods, I recommend you *Forget What You Know About Wheat!* View a whole new world of ingredients from a whole new perspective.   I've learned to embrace the newness. I hope you discover (or re-discover) your own Kitchen Wisdom. From my Kitchen to Yours! Buon Appetito!

Culinary Cultural Evolution

Culinary Cultural Evolution...

Growing up in and around New York City's Italian American neighborhoods of the 1970s, elders had peculiar questions upon meeting someone new. "Where are your parents or grandparents from?" they would ask. The answer was always "*io e Napolitana*" (or the American "I am Neapolitan"); followed by the second question, "What is your last name?" This allowed the seeker to place my people and possibly, my character. In fact, I did not learn to say "Italian" until I was in High School living on Long Island with my mom. This is because, for the Italian immigrants of years ago, identity was part of the particular region of Italy one's family originated. Being from "Italy" was just a geographic expression and lacked actual significance or meaning.

The culinary experiences in this book are a culmination of all of these various Italian and Italian American experiences I have enjoyed. During my generation there was still a notable migration of Italians to New York City and its suburbs. Of course, these Italian immigrants now fly into Kennedy Airport and are often able to live in neighborhoods already financially established, amongst a people already assimilated. The *New World* experienced by my elders was markedly different than the experience of those who arrived in the 1970s and later.

I grew up as Italian American in a *cultural mosaic*; my parents grew up as Italian Americans in a *melting pot*. These are very different sociological terms which reflect the change in American attitudes toward immigration. Many of my parents' generation were not taught our family's native language (Campanian dialect.) This was orchestrated by some elders as a means to ensure success in the dominant American culture of the *New World*. In the *melting pot,* my parents' generation learned that much of the food of our people was considered *"peasant food"*, and many in our community assimilated to the American meat and potatoes diet. Their generation often scoffed at some of the spiritual behaviors of the elders, which Americans considered *superstitious* or not based in the American rational of "scientific" thought. To be successful in the *melting pot* of American society my parents' generation needed to *pass*, rather, they needed to entirely absorb the dominant culture in order to be fruitful in the *New World*. They needed to *melt* into the larger pot of Americanism to guarantee their slice of the American pie.

Living in a *cultural mosaic*, some ethnicities are now socially permitted to maintain much of their culture as an expression of themselves. A number of current immigrant cultures have increased social license to honor their individual heritage, food, superstitions, religions and traditional languages of their ancestors or home country. Years ago, I recall reading that a byproduct of *assimilation* for immigrant descendants in the *New World* is that food becomes the only cultural expression which remains. The food of my people is now my sole reminder of a complex culture my ancestors brought with them, the remaining ingredient - *gastronomy*.

Being a single mom and living at a time where the idea of "day care" was in its infancy, my mom chose to have family members be responsible for me while she worked. This choice was largely influenced by our culture, as Italians and many Italian Americans do not believe *"outsiders"* (those outside of the family) should raise one's children. Our culture is rooted in the importance of *extended family*. It is believed family must all be responsible for our children, how else will they learn the ways of our culture – of our blood?

There, in the kitchens of my elders, I learned to cook in the ways of the *Old World*. In those kitchens I learned early in life how to prepare basic, enriching and inexpensive meals. My elders provided me with love, culture and a sense of belonging. Some elders were born in the *Old Country* and some were born to that special generation of Italian Americans from the 1910s and 1920s. Their existence in my life created a bridge – a bridge built on love, guidance, nurturance and respect. This bridge allowed me to view established traditions. They raised me with a perspective which differs from the average American set of cultural norms and mores.

"*Culture*", with its customary beliefs, social norms, and material traits of a racial, religious or social group[1] has the potential to influence one's sense of self and sense of belonging in and relating to the world. My elders (now my ancestors) offered the culture of my people as a foundation for how I relate in the world. What I take with me of the old is something I have inherited from the past [2], my *heritage*.

I had a beautifully unique opportunity to often be under the care of my grandparents and their siblings. The primary activity with my elders was always preparing the evening meal, and sometimes lunch and breakfast too. Baking was *ritual*. I spent countless hours and beautiful moments with my elders privately in their kitchens. While teaching me particular recipes or baking methods, they would typically teach me life lessons too. I believe this was done with intention.

As I grew to be an adult, cooking and baking have played significant roles in my life. When living on the west coast I decided it was time record my family's traditional ethnic recipes.   My maternal grandmother, Yolanda Ruggiero, had stressed the importance of recording family recipes. I was ultimately given her treasured recipe collections, the recipes of her family as well as my maternal grandfather and her friends. Moving around the country has awakened me to the uniqueness of my culinary experiences over the years. I decided if I wanted to learn more, the generations were passing on, and time was running out. In addition to renewed fervor visiting my own family kitchens, I initiated frequenting the kitchens of many close friends and their families. I began recording and refining recipes like a woman on a mission.

Then I was derailed, or at least I thought I was. I learned I have NCGS and needed to embrace a gluten free lifestyle. On a day plagued with struggles around food, I had an epiphany. "*Forget what I know about wheat*" I said to myself – "that's what I have to do!" *Forgetting what I knew about wheat* meant letting go and re-learning from the beginning. I feel I had resisted acceptance of this new approach was due to a longing for the "deliciousness" of wheat (bread, pasta, pizza, cookies, cakes, etc.) Not being able to prepare or eat many of the foods of my people was a huge adjustment. I was startled to realize the traditional recipes were somehow, part my personal story – a part of who I am.

I began to realize the lessons with my elders had been an inherent part of my self and was somehow integrated into cooking and baking with gluten. I thought I had to surrender the lessons; the moments in time shared in peace, light and love with so many beautiful people in my family. I feared letting go of all of those experiences and the moments shared. I began to understand I needed to look at everything through a different lens, a different perspective. I had no idea I would venture into bold new culinary worlds. I never anticipated the flavors could be so enticing. I was astounded at the potential of gluten free cooking and the wonderful things I was about to learn. This is how *Kitchen Wisdom Gluten Free* was born. This work regards food not only as a substance, but also as a *cultural phenomenon*.

My traditional elders have all passed on. All I have left to offer is my interpretation of the ways of those who came before me. They left me their legacy of love, their recipes and many of their social and moral beliefs They taught me that I am part of something much greater than myself. They passed their culture to me as a foundation for my path in life. It challenges me when I realize all I have left to pass on is my interpretation, my *Cultural Heritage*. These culturally authentic recipes are a part of my ancestors' cultural legacy; transforming these recipes to their enticing Gluten Free complement is an intentional cultural transformation.   I like to call the whole process *Culinary Cultural Evolution*.

Clockwise starting top left: My Conforti's; Yolanda Ruggiero (1940) in Central Park

Cultural Heritage Preservation

The United Nations Educational, Scientific and Cultural Organization (UNESCO), has a World Heritage Centre. The Historic Center of Naples, as well as other sites in Campania are designated UNESCO World Heritage Sites. Naples is one of the most ancient cities in Europe and has hosted its own culture, language and unique gastronomy for the past 2,500 years. According to UNESCO, "*Heritage* is our legacy from the past, what we live with today, and what we pass on to future generations...What makes the concept of World Heritage exceptional is its universal application. World Heritage sites belong to all the peoples of the world, irrespective of the territory on which they are located."[3]

I have chosen to include the gluten rich recipes I was raised with. The gluten rich recipes are presented as a base for comparison and understanding the difference in gluten free baking and how to use gluten free flour combinations.   Their inclusion also fulfills my personal feelings of obligation to preserve and share the gastronomy as part of the *Cultural Heritage,* of those who came before me. Wikipedia states that "*Cultural heritage* is unique and irreplaceable, which places the responsibility of preservation on the current generation."[4]

My anticipation is that *Kitchen Wisdom Gluten Free* will prove to be a very handy and useful reference tool for quick answers on how to bake and cook gluten free. This is a book of Kitchen Wisdom, the wisdom of food and life. I hope you find the stories and the foods pleasing to your palate and your heart.

Forget What You Know about Wheat!

Why are we trying to mimic the taste of gluten rich all-purpose flour?

In "Flour Milling in America," Master Miller Theodore Hazen, describes how the milling process was transformed with the introduction of grains to the *New World*. In Europe, the lord of the land was the possessor of grain mills and those same lords dictated and controlled the peasant's use of the mill. Knowledge of milling was passed from journeyman to apprentice, which allowed for little or no changes to the milling process.

In America, no one was dependent upon the feudal lord for milling and grain supplies. Many American entrepreneurs began to experiment with new technology and power sources. Initially, American mills were driven by human labor and water power. In 1795 Oliver Evans originated the idea that grain and flour could be processed mechanically. These mills only existed along the Northern Atlantic coastline of New England. Gradually, as technology improved, mills were moved inland. Evans' machinery was the beginning of the first automation in an industrial setting.

Flour was not always the white powdery consumer good we are now all familiar with. Milling advanced with the ability to grind wheat into smaller and smaller fragments. In the 1870s, millers in the Minneapolis area created fine flour, most similar to what we recognize today as white flour. To get this fine powder, wheat is stripped of just about all of its nutritional content to provide for lightness and a prolonged shelf life. Back in the 1870s it was difficult to get American housewives to use the flour, as consumer feedback often complained of the flour lacking flavor. Consider for a moment the irony which accompanies our quest to make gluten free baked goods taste like white wheat flour baked goods.

What Makes Wheat So Special and How Does it Work?   Wheat is one of the most versatile grains. Wheat allows one to make high-rise artisanal bread, a dense scone or bar cookie, light and flaky pastry, or use as a thickener as in roux...what can't be made from wheat? A gluten free baked good, that's what! There is no single magical flour combination for gluten free baking. However, that doesn't mean gluten free baking has to be dry, crumbly, lacking in flavor and boring.

What is Gluten?

Wheat, Rye, and Barley all contain a protein composite called gluten. Glutens make up about 80 percent of the protein found in wheat. Gluten contains gliadin and glutenin which work together to create a network (matrix) of cross links which provide structure and elasticity with the addition of water to the flour.

When dough made with wheat flour is kneaded, or batter is mixed, gluten networks form. Like a net, gluten creates air bubbles. Gluten can stretch and trap the bubbles of gas that make the dough or batter rise. Gluten is responsible for springy strands that form in flour when liquid is added. The ability of strands to stretch is an example of gluten in action and is what gives wheat its super versatile abilities. Gluten provides elasticity to batter and dough. Once baked, while the moisture evaporates, gluten becomes rigid which provides the shape for the baked good. Gluten helps batter and dough rise, keep its shape and can even produce a chewy texture (5).

There are differences in gluten content of various baked goods. "Bread flour" has a very high gluten content so that breads can rise high; this is why a light and airy gluten free bread can be a baker's nightmare challenge. "Cake flour" is low in gluten, allowing for better control and less rise in the final baked good. Pie and tart shells use very little gluten. "All Purpose Flour" has a moderate amount of gluten so it is versatile and can accommodate most baked goods recipes. Those of us who grew up baking and eating wheat flour may have taken for granted wheat's diversity and function. This is why I believe so many of us are overwhelmed during first attempts to bake anything gluten free.

Why do we need combinations of other flours and leavening agents to accomplish what wheat accomplishes? Gluten's diversity, versatility and flexibility allow wheat flour to be used for just about anything! To create a gluten free baked good with stable structure, a good crumb and a noticeable rise, we need to get creative and employ a number of ingredients to do the same thing.

Forget what you know about wheat! My anticipation is that this chapter will help you understand how it all works in concert. As previously stated, wheat is the most versatile of all the flours used in baking. This is why white flour is used in just about everything American foods have to offer. For those of us choosing to bake with gluten free flours - we signed on to a seemingly enormous task. Enormous only until the veil of mystery is lifted, until one understands how the ingredients function alone and in combination.

I recommend purchasing flours labeled "gluten free" from a local natural foods store which gets a lot of traffic, this is to ensure better odds on quick product turnaround and freshest possible gluten free flours. Once your flours are purchased, I suggest transferring the flours to mason jars with tight fitting lids. I keep all dry ingredients behind the door of a cool and dark kitchen cabinet. Sunlight bleaches and removes flavor and nutrients from dry ingredients, it also turns oils rancid. Humidity, light and heat will cause herbs and spices to lose their flavor. I never recommend storing anything over the refrigerator as the heat turns food stale and often moldy.

The Gluten Containing Grains:

Wheat, Rye, Barley (and all hybrid forms of these grains) are all gluten containing grains. Some flavorings, sweeteners, and anti-caking agents can be derived from these gluten containing grains. For example, barley is used in *malt* and sometimes in smoke flavor. Rye is sometimes used in flavorings. Due to crop rotations many grains which naturally occur as gluten free ultimately test positive for gluten contamination. Be sure to always purchase grains which say "gluten free."

Types of Wheat: *Kamut* is the most ancient wheat species; *Durum* is a type of wheat which is ground into *Semolina*; *Spelt* (faro); Einkorn wheat; *Triticale* is a hybrid of rye and wheat.

Gluten Containing Foods: The FDA recommends reading the Ingredient Statement on the label of any food product purchased (6). Knowing what chemicals or agents are in your diet, is critical for someone with issues around gluten. Obvious gluten rich foods are bread, crackers, cookies, muffins and pizza. Less obvious, however are *Hidden Glutens*. Some salad dressings, chocolates, gravies, condiments, candy and many prepared foods in general. It can be shocking, and educational, to discover the myriad of foods that contain an origin in wheat and or gluten.

"Gluten Free" Labeling in the US

The idea that wheat needed to be included as an allergen was passed into the US Food Allergen Labeling & Consumer Protection Act (FALCPA) in 2004. Title II of Public Law 208 asserts that wheat is an allergen and advisory statements need to be included on labels. It also required that gluten containing source ingredients be listed on the ingredient statement of each label. When "Food Labeling" was amended to include wheat, FALCPA provided the FDA with limited gluten free labeling guidelines which instructed manufacturers and food processors the following: *if wheat gluten is present in the formulation of foods, flavorings, extracts and colorings, then the source grain needs to be listed on the ingredient statement*(7). The law also instructed the FDA to come up with a rule defining and permitting use of the term "gluten free" for labeling (8).

In August of 2013, the FDA issued a final rule regarding gluten free labeling for food and diet supplements. Any person who is documented as suffering from CD or NCGS and has a reaction to something labeled "gluten free" must go to their doctor and have their doctor confirm the reaction is from exposure. Then the individual can report the incident to the FDA Compliance officer in the state the food was eaten. The FDA labeling of gluten in pharmaceuticals is yet to come; it will be a separate rule and is under consideration at the time of this writing.

The advent of the new gluten free labeling law is designed to settle what products can be considered "gluten free". The rule went into effect in September of 2013, but the compliance date is August 4, 2014. This means food manufacturers have until August of 2014 to change labels and review all ingredients in their products. The FDA's online Q&A regarding "gluten free" labeling states, "...the FDA anticipates manufacturers are likely to follow the requirements of the final rule as soon as possible.(9)" The rule is clear and we now have a USDA definition of "gluten free". Across the food industry, gluten free claims are now standardized. Included in the "gluten free" terminology are claims which state: "no gluten", "free of gluten" and "without gluten". To be labeled "gluten free" foods must be inherently gluten free, or not contain an ingredient that is a gluten containing ingredient or is derived from a gluten containing grain that has not been processed to remove gluten or derived from a gluten containing grain that has been processed to remove gluten if the use of that ingredient results in the presence of 20ppm (parts per million) of gluten in the food(10). This means no food labeled "gluten free" can contain more than 19ppm of gluten. So now it is clear for consumers - or is it? PPM, parts per million, is a parts per notation set of "pseudo units to describe small values of miscellaneous dimensionless quantities in science and engineering.(11)" It is a measurement of something which is microscopic; one cannot see the 19ppm of gluten residing on food. The US and EU (European Union) use CODEX method for measurement. There are other measurement methods available and these are what independent groups (like GFCO) use.

Contacting manufacturers reveals differences and similarities manufacturers are using for labeling. Food companies, such as Heinz mention in email correspondence with me that "...recipes can change without notice. Therefore, we recommend you always check the ingredient statement on the label.(12)" Lawry's uses "'Plain English' allergen labeling to communicate [their] product ingredients. When gluten is present as an ingredient,[Lawry's] will always declare it as "wheat" or "barley" in the ingredient statement.(13)" Lawry's is a McCormick company and McCormick has the same thing to say about all of their products.(14)

8 Allergens & US Food Label Advisories: FALCPA (Food Allergen Labeling & Consumer Protection Act of 2004) designates the following foods as major food allergens: milk, eggs, fish, crustacean shellfish, tree nuts, peanuts, wheat and soybeans. [15]   Labels which alert consumers that the product was made in a facility which also processes wheat, are such an advisory. The FDA refers to cross contamination as "Cross Contact" and they recognize it is an issue in facilities which package and manufacture foods with the various allergens. If you use a particular packaged food product and are concerned about it containing gluten or its subjectivity to cross contamination, I encourage you to email or call the food manufacturer in question.

Hidden Gluten in Food Additives: At the time of this writing some forms of Modified Food Starch; Hydrolyzed Wheat Gluten; Hydrolyzed Wheat Protein; Hydrolyzed Wheat Protein Pg-Propyl Silanetriol; Hydrolyzed Wheat Starch; Hydroxypropyltrimonium Hydrolyzed Wheat Protein; Stearyldimoniumhydroxypropyl Hydrolyzed Wheat Protein; Hydrolyzed Plant Protein; Hydrolyzed Protein; Hydrolyzed Vegetable Protein; Hydrogenated Starch Hydrolysate; Hydroxypropylated Starch; Maltose; Modified Food Starch; Modified Starch; Non-dairy Creamer; Pregelatinized Starch; Protein Hydrolysates; TVP (texturized vegetable protein).[16]

Are Distilled Spirits Gluten Free?

Distillation is a process by which ethanol is produced by fermenting grain, fruit or vegetables. The source is fermented, heated and the fermented alcohol (ethanol) is captured, leaving the fermented grain, fruit or vegetable behind. Distilled and fermented products which are made from gluten containing source grains and are processed, treated or crafted to remove gluten cannot be labeled "Gluten Free" in the United States. We Have seen this enforcement over the past two years. At the time of this writing in 2014: Absolut, Jack Daniels and other brands follow EU standards and claim their clean spirits without flavoring (e.g. Vodka as opposed to Vanilla Vodka) are free of gluten. Many of these brands make statements like Absolut: "the gluten is removed in the production process...(17) or Jack Daniels "...it is generally recognized...that distilled alcoholic beverages, including bourbons and whiskies, are gluten-free, because the gluten is not carried over in the distillation process."(18) Distilled Spirits Manufacturers of this perspective generally cite the EU Food Law EC/178/2002 and its subsequent amendments. However, a closer look at EU regulation reveals something unsettling. The EU (by regulation) uses a private corporation, European Food Safety Authority (EFSA), to provide "independent scientific advice" on questions of foods and food safety. In 2007 EFSA provided an opinion for a "permanent exemption"(19) from allergen status on distilled spirits originating from gluten containing grains. To draw this conclusion, EFSA's research used only "current literature"(20) on the topic and "analytical data(21) on potential residual proteins (gluten.) EFSA did not conduct clinical studies on humans and EFSA did not use double blind placebo controlled food challenge clinical studies. Yet, EFSA concluded that it is "unlikely"(22) distillates made from gluten containing grains elicit a severe allergic reaction. EFSA also concluded that proteins (gluten) are not carried over into distillate during properly controlled distillation process.

In the United States on August 2, 2013 the US FDA (Food & Drug Administration) issued a rule regarding gluten free labeling of foods and drugs. The FDA does not regulate alcohol beverages; the (TTB) Alcohol & Tobacco Tax & Trade Bureau (of the US Department of the Treasury) regulates alcohol. The TTB announced in May 2012, "...a ruling providing guidelines for labeling alcohol beverages with gluten content claims."(23) The ruling was issued "because products made from ingredients that contain gluten may, despite processing to remove gluten, still contain gluten that cannot be detected using available testing methods."(24)

What does this mean for those of us who can't consume gluten? Don't use the extract nor drink the alcohol in question until you know the source grain. If the source grain has gluten, you may have a reaction. You can email customer service for just about any distilled spirit on the market. I encourage you to ask directly which of their products are gluten free, and what guideline do they use to determine the presence of gluten.

Flavored spirits are becoming more and more popular. I enjoy the occasional mixed drink, but have felt very left out of this current trend. As previously mentioned, many food additives are derived from source grains which include gluten. This includes flavorings, colorings, extracts and stabilizers. Contacting the manufacturer is the only way to learn for sure if your favorite drink has gluten.

Gluten Free Ingredients & Handling: The Gluten Free market was highly scrutinized in 2004. It has shown annual growth of 28% for the last four years. Industry projections estimate $6.6 Billion in industry wide earnings in 2017(25). Companies, restaurants, or any food purveyor dedicated to conventional palates, would be wise to learn the particulars of gluten free food preparation and handling. (26) Many natural food brands are dedicated to the purity of their product by using gluten free processing facilities in addition to gluten free ingredients. Some companies have gone beyond the basics of the FDA law and are producing foods with GCFCO certification. GFCO is a very strict certifying body and is a not-for-profit organization, separate and distinct from the Federal Government. Their scrutiny recognizes 10ppm is the threshold. (27)

Cross Contact in the Kitchen

Home and professional kitchens that prepare gluten free and gluten rich foods need to follow certain steps to reduce cross contamination. It is critical to understand that a negative reaction can occur to even the smallest amount of gluten particulate matter. Wheat flour particulate matter takes 24 hours to settle, which means when you walk into a kitchen the morning after bread was baked – you are being exposed to gluten via inhalation.

I need to interject - there is a broad spectrum of symptoms concerning sensitivity to gluten. As discussed earlier, CD is an auto-immune disease triggered by inhalation, ingestion and digestion of gluten. NCGS is an immune system response to the presence of gluten. The level to which the exposure to gluten affects our lives seems to be very different person to person. Wheat Allergy is an immune system response which can end in Anaphylaxis. CD & NCGS symptoms can range from gastrointestinal issues, but many more have other types of issues: menstrual issues, earaches, depression, eczema, anaphylactic shock, anxiety, etc.

In our own kitchens, we hopefully exercise as much gluten free control as possible. But when we eat out, we are truly at the mercy of the establishment and their particular dedication to limiting or restricting cross contact of proteins during ingredient handling. Some are very responsible and dedicated to reducing cross contact, some are not.

GIG (Gluten Intolerance Group), the organization responsible for GFCO GF Certification, has the following recommendations: Keep flours in separate containers in separate cabinets. Don't use the same cutting boards, wooden and metal spoons, utensils pans, mixing bowls, pot holders, dish towels, sponges. If you use a kitchen smock, have designated clothing for gluten free and gluten rich preparations. Clean everything in hot wet soapy water.(28) Always use hot water and pay close attention to this cycle: rinse, scrub, rinse, thoroughly dry. Use of hot water is the best way to remove gluten from surfaces and helps to reduce cross contamination in the kitchen. Concerning cross contamination from grains which are part of wheat crop rotations, cross contamination can begin on the farm. For more information please read in this chapter, below "Is That Gluten Free Grain Gluten Free?"

Eating Out? Beware of Cross Contact!

Cross Contact of proteins and hidden gluten is the enemy when eating out. I recommend you have a conversation with your server about gluten free. Ask if the restaurant has any special menu items or a gluten free menu. (Remember, restaurants choose to offer items or menus without gluten, and at this time, most states do not have professional restaurant kitchen regulations on gluten free practices & procedures.) Examples of Cross Contact include salads or vegetables prepared on a board contaminated by croutons or bread. If you are getting something fried, ask if there is a dedicated gluten free fryolator.   Is there a coating on food you are ordering? If so, what are the coating ingredients? One should consider the possibility wheat flour or a gluten containing condiment was used in the sauce on your entrée. Ask that your food not be prepared on a grill or any cooking surface shared with gluten rich ingredients, I always request my burgers be cooked individually in its own pan. Ask about salad dressings and/or marinades used in your selection ... these are a huge source of hidden gluten. Also consider that soups and sauces often have a wheat flour base or use a bullion or condiment which contains gluten.

Condiments & Hidden Gluten

Reading ingredient statements on food is at the core of gluten free living. Many flavorings use a wheat base, many colorings use a malt (barley) base, and condiments often use wheat or gluten containing source grains to create a thick or gravy texture. Consequently, careful consideration should be given to choosing condiments. I suggest keeping a list of gluten containing ingredients and suspect additives, until you become accustomed to what additives you are trying to avoid. Email your favorite condiment manufacturers and ask them directly for a gluten free product list.

Some spice manufacturers use anti-caking agents, if the anti-caking agent has a wheat source it is supposed to be listed. Steak Sauces are a huge source of hidden glutens; Asian Sauces, like Duck, Plum, and Hoison, Sriracha often have hidden gluten. I find many condiment companies are very happy to answer questions about gluten and manufacturing; many products are gluten free and produced in facilities that don't process wheat. French Fries & Various Prepackaged Potatoes are often plagued with hidden gluten – this is especially true in restaurants! If the fryolator isn't dedicated gluten free, those fries are not gluten free. Coatings are generally a culprit, many manufacturers use wheat.

Checking your *chocolate* is crucial. Most chocolate contains either soy lecithin (a natural emulsifier) or barley malt. Soy is subject to cross contact issues at the seed level. A lot of candies use wheat as a thickener and stabilizer. Many brands of marshmallows use some form of wheat.   Many Alcohol Mixers have hidden or direct gluten. I always recommend learning how to make the drink from scratch.

Let's touch on *Soy* for a moment. Soy is a rotation crop for wheat and is often contaminated with gluten. Soy Sauce in the American marketplace is almost always exposed to gluten, specifically wheat. I recommend using Tamari that says it is from a gluten free source. Some soy milk contains barley malt or soy from rotated crops. At the time of this writing, there are no available brands of soy flour on the market which are gluten free. "Wheat free" is not "gluten free", be very careful when choosing ingredients.

Store bought Salad Dressings, Marinades & BBQ Sauces: Homemade salad dressings are actually quite easy to make and store well. Beware of "smoke" and "liquid smoke" as it is often made from malt (barley).   Email food manufacturers with question about processing, if necessary.

Vinegar: Clear Vinegars are often made from malt or wheat derivatives, Mustard is often made with malt (barley) vinegar. Red or white wine vinegars are generally free from gluten containing ingredients, but always check the label or contact the manufacturer. Some Apple Cider Vinegars are also gluten free.

As delicious as wheat had been in my previous daily diet, I find the spectrum of new flavors available in gluten free flours to be far more exciting and enticing! *Kitchen Wisdom* demonstrates the belief anyone interested in cooking or baking gluten free can learn to do so and it need not be a difficult transition.

Is that Gluten Free Grain Gluten Free?

Gluten free flours are ground from various starchy plants: grassy cereal grains, plant grains, seed grain, beans and roots. They provide bulk to baked items. They have a diverse range of protein content. They are best used in combination - no individual gluten free flour is as diverse and flexible as flour which contains gluten (wheat, barley and rye). The naturally occurring gluten free grains and starches are: rice, corn, potato, tapioca, bean/legume flours, sorghum, arrowroot, amaranth, quinoa, millet, teff, flax, chia, and nut flours. *However,* many naturally gluten free grains are subject to crop rotation or processed on equipment shared with wheat. Therefore *cross contact* is a huge concern. Always make sure the label states the flour is gluten free.

I have come across references to research done on grains which are considered inherently gluten free. Due to crop rotations, gluten free grain seeds co-mingle with gluten containing seeds and gluten particulate matter in the soil. The Celiac Awareness Campaign of the US National Institutes of Health, in the *Study Finds Gluten Contamination of Inherently Gluten-free Grains and Flours*, "researchers tested 22 inherently gluten-free grains, seeds, and flours that were not labeled gluten-free, including millet, white rice flour, buckwheat, soy flour, basmati rice, corn meal, and flax seed" (29) it goes on to say that *32% of grains considered to be inherently gluten free have tested positive for glutens.* Therefore the statement, "oh that's a gluten free grain" is misleading. Just because a grain naturally occurs as gluten free in its most pure and naked state, does not mean it is grown on land free from gluten contamination and it does not mean it was processed in gluten free facilities. This is the intersection of why so many products cannot make gluten free claims under the new FDA gluten free labeling law.

After sharing this information with my friend his response was, "You wonder why a lot of people with Celiac Disease never get well after so many years of going gluten free, all of these gluten free grains which get contaminated in the fields and in the processing; it is best to use whole foods and companies we can trust (29b)." This should underscore how prevalent gluten is in our food supply.

GMO (Genetically Modified Organisms): Dr. Tina D'Amato had a conversation with me recently. She asked me about my gluten free eating habits. She wanted to know if I eat a lot of corn, because people diagnosed with CD or NCGS tend to eat more corn and soy products which are the most common GMO foods in the American food supply. At the time I was consuming a lot of corn flour and related products, I often use corn tortillas as wraps. Tortilla chips are also a common item in kitchen. She asked me if I was eating organic and/or non-GMO corn. She warned me about the dangers of "BT toxin." GMO corn contains a toxin which pokes holes in the intestines of insects; the idea is the plant can protect itself without the addition of pesticides. However, recent studies have shown the toxin has the ability to poke microscopic holes in the intestines of humans. There is a theory that food allergies have erupted parallel to the growth of GMO foods in our food supply and the hypothesized reason for the increase in food allergies is related to this action of BT toxin on the intestines. Remember, just because a food is labeled "gluten free" does not mean it has not been genetically engineered. (30). What does all of this mean? I went home and threw out my conventional tortillas. At this time GMO foods do not have to be labeled as such, and the burden is on the consumer to look for GMO free statements on the label.

A quick note about the term *"glutinous"* and corn or rice: "glutinous" refers to the glue like chemical reaction these grains have when soaked in water or exposed to hot water. *Glutinous* in this sense has nothing to do with the protein *gluten* found naturally occurring in wheat, rye and barley.

Gluten Free Flours

Buckwheat:

- Not related to wheat, is not a grass and does not contain gluten.

- Usually grown as a cover crop, it has a fruit which looks like a seed. It is sometimes called Kasha. In its whole form the fruit is also ground into flour. Raw kasha is delicious on salad. As a flour it has a nutty flavor and is excellent in crepes.

Ceci/Chickpea/Garbanzo Bean Flour:

- High in protein with very strong flavor and it imparts a bitter after taste in baked goods. I recommend using this flour in cooking. If used in baking, use in moderation and in combination with sorghum, which can weaken the aftertaste.

- Indian markets sell this flour as *Gram flour* or *Besan*. *Chana dal* are chickpeas. Be sure they are labeled as gluten free and not processed in a facility which processes wheat.

- Delicious when used as a thickener in gravies, stews and chili; imparts enjoyable flavor as flour for dredging cutlets.

Coconut:

- Coconut is not a nut, rather it is a drupe. The fruit of the coconut is actually a seed. The flesh, oil and milk are used for cooking. It is from a Palm tree and not a member of the Tree Nut family.

- It is very high in fiber and its fat content can help make cookies crispy.

Corn Flours

Corn flours are plant grain, available in different milled textures, ranging from course to fine. I recommend using masa harina for baking, it is very fine and light - it is excellent in dredged coatings. A very coarse grind of corn flour, Polenta, is also a traditional Northern Italian dish made of the same named corn flour. I use polenta cornmeal in some gluten free breadcrumb recipes.

Masa Harina:

• Made from yellow or white corn (maize) and is very light and much like flour. It is the main ingredient in tamales and tortillas. It is an important flour in Mexican cooking. Corn is soaked in water with lime (not the fruit) to soften the kernels and loosen the husks. It is then rinsed, dried and pulverized.

• I use it in combination with other flours for some baked goods. It can make a baked good taste like corn, so it needs to be used in moderation.

• Delicious as a thickener in gravies, stews and chili and as a light coating in dredging.

Polenta:

• It is ground yellow or white corn and is a grade of very coarsely textured cornmeal.

• Excellent for cooking entrees which require a thicker coating. Use it in with other flours in some gluten free breadcrumb mixtures.

Millet:

- Very high in protein, it is a grass and naturally occurs as gluten free.

- It is flavorful and contributes moisture to recipes, it is a wonderful addition to a pancake batter.

Nut & Seed Meal

Nut and Seed meal (slightly coarse grind of the nut) can be made by placing whole or sliced nuts in food processor. Some commercially produced nut meals are made from residue remaining from the nut oil extraction process. When processing nut meal, pulse nuts for a few seconds periodically. The texture becomes meal – create a texture appropriate for the recipe. Pulse quickly and intermittently, nut meals turn to nut butters quickly if you are not paying close attention. When processing nut meal for a recipe, I usually process additional and store it a jar with tight fitting lid in the fridge for future use. I use Pignoli (Pine nuts) and Hazelnuts regularly; however, their costs prohibit using many cups in recipes as meal and are therefore not included.

Almonds:

- Very high in minerals, Vitamin E and Folate and high in monounsaturated and polyunsaturated fats. Almonds are high in protein.

Almond Flour:

- Almonds are processed to fine flour, not a meal. Available in most natural foods markets, however be cautious of rancidity. Nuts release oils which can become rancid very quickly when exposed to oxygen and heat during the grinding process.

• It can be difficult to get correct light and fluffy texture at home; this texture is best purchased at a natural food store (none of the recipes in this book use the ultra-light and fluffy meal.)

Almond Meal:

• Made from blanched or unblanched almonds. The skin can contribute additional nutrients to a textural baked good but it is not recommended for light recipes.

• Delicious as a flour for dredging. It's very high protein content makes it an excellent addition to baked good gluten free flour combinations for baked goods.

Sesame Seeds:

• One of the most ancient foods known to humans; It imparts a warm and subtle low on the palate – sort of a "what is that mystery flavor?" flavor.

• High in Oleic Acid (Omega 6 Fatty Acid) and high in essential minerals and Folic Acid. Added to salad, sesame seeds are a delicious way to increase protein.

• I grind in a spice mill and use as sesame flour in coatings and breadcrumbs; can also be used as a thickener in stews.

Walnuts:

• High in phosphorous, magnesium, potassium and protein. They are predominantly composed of polyunsaturated fatty acids (omega 3 and omega 6). They oxidize quickly, so once shelled, chopped or halved they should be kept in an airtight container in the refrigerator or freezer.

- The Black Walnut is indigenous to North and South America.

- It is delicious in combination with sorghum as a flour for dredging.

- It is delicious as a flour to use when making cupcakes and cakes with vegetables (like carrot cake).

Oats:

- Naturally occur as gluten free, however, they have been subject to gluten cross contact from neighboring fields and crop rotations with wheat. Be sure to purchase certified gluten free oats.

Potato Flour:

- Not to be confused with potato starch.

- It can have a strong flavor and should be used this way: 1-2 tablespoons per 2-3 cups of gluten free flour combination.

- It is made from skin on, cooked potatoes. Then it is dried and finely ground. Some may call it a secret ingredient in gluten free baking as it provides moisture for gluten free flours in baking.

- It can also be used as a thickener.

- Used in large quantities, it imparts a slight potato flavor.

Quinoa:

• An edible seed grain that is high in protein. In whole form it is a delicious substitute for rice in your favorite recipes.

• When used as a flour it imparts a mild nutty flavor.

Rice Flours

The recipes in this book use both white and brown rice flours. If a light as possible color is desired, then white rice flour is the answer. White more closely mimics the color we have become accustomed to seeing on finished wheat based baked goods. If not used in correct combination with other flours it will impart a grainy texture. Potato Starch and Arrowroot are excellent starches to use with rice flour and they each cut that grittiness (graininess) of the rice flour. Once the grit is cut, the finished product is smooth.

Brown Rice Flour:

• Brown rice flour has a high nutritional content. It has a mild to neutral flavor.

• Brown rice flour has the bran and should be kept as fresh as possible, it stores in a heavy, airtight container kept in dark and cool location up to three months.

• It is gritty and must be used in combination with a starch (like potato starch or arrowroot) to soften the grit and render it unnoticeable once baked.

Sweet Rice Flour:

• Made from "Sticky Rice" and is *glutinous* and it is gluten free (*glutinous* refers to it having a much higher starch content). The high starch content makes it an excellent thickener and binder.

• It has little or no flavor and adopts flavors of other ingredients in batter or dough, it has a super finely ground. All of the bran has been removed.

• Excellent for feather light batters and pastry dough. Wonderful in combination with other starches when duplicating the look of airy and light white wheat baked goods.

White Rice Flour:

• Rice which is milled and has the bran removed. The bran is the nucleus of the grain and it contains "impurities" that can go rancid. The "impurities" are mainly fats and protein as well as many vitamins and minerals. White Rice has a longer shelf life due to its lacking in "impurities."

• It is gritty and must be used in combination with a starch (like potato starch or arrowroot) to soften its grit and make it unnoticeable once baked.

• It has neutral flavor.

Sorghum Flour:

• A species of grass raised for grain.

• Closest to wheat in flavor, carbohydrates, protein, fat and fiber; its addition adds a wheat like familiar bottom flavor in baked goods.

• Too much creates a dry product and needs to have correct moisture content to have a successful baked good. I highly recommend its use and it can be used very well in combination with other flours. Be warned: if you use too much, the product may be too crumbly or dry.

• Also called "jowar" or "juwar" and available at Indian markets, be sure they are labeled as gluten free and not processed in a facility which processes wheat.

• Can sweeten (and sometimes remove) the bitterness or aftertaste from Cici (chickpea/garbanzo) flour in cooking and baking.

Soy Flour:

• At the time of this writing, there are no companies which offer gluten free soy flour. Soy is a rotated crop with wheat and subject to cross contamination in the field and during handling and processing. Tofu and soy milk are available gluten free, but you must read "gluten free" on the label to be sure.

Teff:

• Teff is a cereal grass originally from Africa. It is high in fiber, protein, calcium and iron. In the US it is often used in wheat crop rotation and therefore subject to cross contamination and must be gluten free certified.

Gluten Free Starches

The following gluten free flours provide bulk and aid in binding ingredients together. They assist in structure formation of the final baked good. They are bland and are best used in combination with other flours to maximize nutrient content and flavor of final baked good.

Arrowroot:

• Arrowroot is a rhizome from the roots of various tropical plants. The Japanese variety is called Kudzu. American variety is from Florida and has various Latin plant names. Natural food stores carry this item in bulk or prepackaged.

• Softens the grittiness of rice flour and is therefore an excellent pairing with brown or white rice flour in baking.

• It contributes to a baked good being light (as in sponge cake) and has a bland flavor.

• Makes clear fruit gels and prevents ice crystals from forming in ice cream.

• Has very little nutritional value apart from carbohydrate. It has almost no protein and therefore must be used in combination with other gluten free flours to create a successful and delicious baked good.

• It contains considerably more calcium and much less sodium than cornstarch and is an excellent substitute for cornstarch in many recipes. It works very well as a thickening agent; however, when used in food cooking, it will NOT reheat to form structure again. Once it becomes watery, it remains watery.

Corn Starch:

• It is easy to find and inexpensive. It can be used in very much the same way as other starches. It is an ingredient used in cooking, baking and has industrial applications. It is often from genetically engineered (GMO) corn, so I recommend a Non GMO Certified product for purchase.

• It is a starch from the casing (endosperm) of the corn kernel. It is slightly sweet, but mostly bland in flavor. In baking it works best paired with Tapioca starch.

• It is used in the packaged food industry as a thickening agent in sauces, gravies, soups and other liquid based products. Also a sweetener, high fructose corn syrup is made from corn starch.

Potato Starch:

• A starch extracted from potatoes. It is an excellent addition to foods which must maintain structure when reheated.

• It reduces grittiness of brown and white rice flour and is especially delicious used in combination with brown rice flour.

• It contributes to a baked good having a light consistency (as in sponge cake). It is bland in flavor, low in fiber and nutrients, has no protein.

• Helps retain moisture and combines well with eggs.

Tapioca:

• It has a starchy, sweet flavor and it is the starch extracted from cassava root.

• I recommend using this floury starch sparingly in baking. It imparts chewyness. It softens the grittiness of rice flour.

• It contributes to a baked good being light (as in sponge cake).

• Can improve color and sweetness of crusts.

• It is used as a thickening agent in cooking. It works very well in gravy.

• It is a main staple of cooking in various parts of Asia and India. Pearl tapioca is used to make *tapioca pudding* as well as many Asian drinks (like Bubble Tea).

The Building Blocks of Baking

I believe we can all learn how to transform our favorite gluten rich recipes to gluten free. It need not be shrouded in mystery. My intention is to help you feel more confident transforming recipes on your own. Remember to be patient; some recipes need to be tweaked more than others. Knowing what ingredients work together and how to use them is important, but understanding how baking is accomplished – the chemistry of baking – is pinnacle.

Even Heating and Accurate Oven Temperature

• Affects both the texture and the look of the cake. Even heating determines how long the batter will take to set. The longer it takes the eggs, milk and flour to coagulate, the more time air cells in the batter have to grow larger and produce increased volume in the cake.

• An oven which is too hot will make the outer edges of cake set sooner than the center, which will produce an over-baked outer edge. An oven which is too cold will yield an under-baked item. Uneven temperature yields an unevenly baked item.

• The oven should always be preheated, by at least 15 minutes before baking the item. I generally turn the oven on at the start of preparing for the recipe. Hanging an oven thermometer in the oven will report the actual heating capacity of the oven.

The Building Blocks of Baking

Gluten free baking strives to mimic the many accomplishments of gluten rich baking: familiar texture, well risen product, texturally soft and moist. Understanding how wheat's most important protein, gluten, functions as a building block in baking is key to creating the best performing and best tasting gluten free baked good. When dough or batter is mixed, the starch in the flour combines with moisture to form a matrix of links that provide structure and elasticity. A gluten rich matrix relies heavily on gluten to accomplish matrix formation. Wheat has high gluten content and therefore does not have to work hard to accomplish this matrix. Gluten free baking is an exploration into the creation of this matrix using ingredients which do not contain the magic of gluten. Understanding how to manipulate gluten free ingredients to maximize protein bonds and strength (or tenderness) is the apex of truly understanding how to make quality gluten free baked goods.

I have read and experienced a lot about how to bake gluten free. Many people seem, in one way or another, to build upon the foundation that Bette Hagman laid for us. Bette Hagman, our "Gluten Free Gourmet", has passed on, but in the 1990's and early 2000's she produced baked goods which were gluten free and tasty. Bette was the Ambassador for the idea that baked goods can be made gluten free. Her work taught us that baked goods need protein as well as gluten like substances in order to rise and have structure. Her main formula is that one needs to maximize protein content via combinations of flour and the addition of protein rich ingredients (such as milk or eggs.) She also taught to supplement for the function of gluten by adding additional ingredients, such as a natural gum (xanthan gum, guar gum or locust bean gum). Natural gums provide elasticity, height and springy-ness to baked goods. They do this as a leavener but must be used in combination with another leavener (like baking powder or baking soda). (31) She painstakingly and laboriously experimented with protein, gluten free flours, leavener, etc... She carved out new frontiers in the kitchen for those of us who cannot consume gluten. Kitchen Wisdom looks to continue to forge those new frontiers in gluten free cooking and baking.

Kitchen Wisdom includes a major departure from use of flour blends in the structure of a recipe. Some recipe developers use flour blends and apply them in different ways; I use similar gluten free flours in similar applications. I do not believe in creating a large flour blend which sits in a cabinet and often goes rancid before using its entirety. I also believe the ingredients list of recipes should identify each ingredient with their corresponding measurement. I list each ingredient with measurement separately for each recipe.

While it is true that wheat and gluten have versatility no other single grain can compete with. That doesn't mean one cannot make delicious gluten free baked goods. Forget what you know about "all purpose" white (wheat) flour, and you will transition into baking with gluten free flours quite nicely. Consider for a moment, Pastry Chefs and Bakers who work with Wheat flours do not use "all purpose" white (wheat) flour for every baking application. For example, the "cake flour" that most professionals use, has low protein and low gluten. The "all purpose" flour seems to have been created for mass consumption in home kitchens, not for finicky home cooks or trained professionals.

When experimenting with converting baking recipes from full gluten to gluten free one must consider: a. the amount of protein in the ingredients; b. the combination of gluten like leavener required to accomplish the desired structure of the baked good; and c. how to maximize nutritional content. Gluten itself is a protein found in wheat. But this is not the only protein found in wheat. Wheat is relatively high in protein in general, the most processed of which yields approximately 13 grams of protein per cup. In general, it is important to be sure any gluten free batters and dough have at least 10 grams or more of protein. I call this the *protein rich approach*.

When choosing gluten free flour combinations remember to use the protein rich approach by maximizing nutrient content with bulk and starch. In the human body, carbohydrates are turned into short term energy as fuel. I believe in choosing one's carbohydrate carefully. I prefer carbohydrates which maximize nutrient and protein content and offer beautiful flavor in combination when baked. Keep in mind, protein in the flour helps to enhance and enforce structure. Once chosen, sift the flours together in a bowl and place aside. Using gluten free flours begins with the evaluation of the overall flavor and desired look of the final baked good.

Strong flavored baked goods I recommend: 10-20% strong flavor flour + 50 percent neutral flavor flour + 30-40% bland flavor (starch)

Mild flavored baked goods I recommend: 60% neutral flavor flour + 40% bland flavor flour (starch)

Pastries and very light and airy baked goods I recommend: 70% bland flavor flour (starch) + 30% neutral flavor flour

Protein's Key Attributes of Protein in baking:

• Protein bond creation favors a more acidic environment (like the use of baking powder in a recipe). This is what commercial dough enhancers accomplish.

• Sugar helps to stabilize protein bonds in baked goods. Stabilizing acts to tenderize and soften the baked good.

• Milk Solids have a binding effect on protein, increasing toughness of a baked good.

• Fats coat the proteins, which water proofs them, making the protein strands slippery so the carbon dioxide gas bubbles can move easily. This lubrication makes dough more pliable.

• Egg protein coagulates during baking and helps flour as a structure builder.

• In gluten free baking, *elasticity* (springiness) in a baked good is increased by the use of a combination of leavener (for example, baking powder plus guar or xanthan gum). In gluten rich baking, the gluten itself creates elasticity. A quick example is when you add liquid to wheat flour and mix with your hand. When you move your fingers in the flour, long strands form. The strands are the action of gluten.

Proteins are found in many gluten free flours, eggs, soy and nut milks, unflavored gelatin, eggs, seeds, nuts and nut butters, and cow's milk dairy products. *Protein in baked goods provides and creates the foundation for structure, texture and elasticity.*

Eggs – Whole: Egg protein coagulates during baking and helps flour as a structure builder, therefore increasing the egg in a recipe will help the cake hold together better. Eggs are a powerful binder.

• If fat is increased in a recipe then eggs generally should be increased as well to sustain the weight.

• Eggs help to regulate toughening action of a baked good.

• Whole eggs add flavor and add springy-ness to bread.

• Eggs can act as a leavening agent. Eggs can provide leavening qualities to soufflés and sponge cakes; they help the items rise high.

• To yield the best volume for batter or dough, it is best to not use cold eggs directly from the refrigerator. This volume is achieved with room temperature eggs because the protein bonds in the eggs are more relaxed and ready to bind flours. Leave fresh eggs on counter for 30 minutes before baking.

Egg White:

• Whipped egg white folded into a batter can provide structure, stability air and volume. Egg Foam is also called Whipping.

• Egg white structure is 7/8 water, 1/8 protein, 0 fat; and contains niacin, riboflavin, chorine, magnesium (as does the yolk). Two medium or three small egg whites = 1 whole egg.

Egg Yolk: is responsible for emulsifying batter. The emulsifier is lecithin in the yolk. When we emulsify we suspend one liquid in another. An emulsifier is a stabilizer.

• Contributes to a fine texture. It also contributes to overall moisture of a cake, making it creamier and smoother.

• Yolk in bread batter can bind and help improve the texture and flavor.

• Egg Yolk beaten with small amount of sugar increases air in the batter.

• Egg Yolk has less than half the protein of a whole egg, but it has more vitamins than egg white. Egg yolk structure is ½ water, 1/6 protein and 1/3 fat. Yolk contains the egg's vitamins A, D, E and zinc. Egg Yolk has 231mg of cholesterol. The American Heart Association recommends no greater than 300mg of cholesterol per day (32).

"Egg Replacer":

• Is not egg and does NOT replace protein of eggs.

• Is a product primarily for the vegan market designed to bind like eggs in baking. It is not always Gluten Free and you must be sure to check package.

• Can provide additional leavening to a gluten free baked good.

Milk:

• Contributes moisture and overall protein level of a baked good.

• Cow's milk and (non-flavored) soy milk can be used as an equal volume for volume exchange.

• I encourage you to experiment with plant based milks (like nut milks, soymilk, rice milk and coconut milk). Each plant has its own fat content and different stabilizers and additives are used dependent upon brand.

Unflavored Gelatin:

• A very strong structure builder, is excellent for pizza and biscuit recipes.

• Can increase moisture in a baked good.

• Made from bone marrow of food industry animals and is not vegetarian.

Fats in Baking

Fats increase the carbon dioxide gas holding ability of dough by coating the flour fibers in batter. Fats coat flour particles, water proofing them. This waterproofing makes the protein strands slippery so the carbon dioxide gas bubbles can move easily on the slippery surface. This lubrication makes dough more pliable.

- When butter is removed or reduced, it increases the chances that the end product will lack flavor and be tough.

- When butter is increased in a recipe, then the eggs must be increased as well.

- I never use Crisco or any other mass produced "shortening." These are comprised of hydrogenated fats, also called trans-fats. The hydrogenation process chemically infuses hydrogen molecules into end products of fats which are solid. The addition of the hydrogen creates a liquid from a solid. Hydrogenated fats are just a few chemical processes away from becoming a plastic. Hydrogenation and trans-fats change the unsaturated and essential fatty acids present in natural oil. Hydrogenated fat contains unnatural fatty acid fragments and other altered molecules, some of which may be toxic. Trans-fats raise low density lipoproteins (LDL – bad cholesterol) levels just as saturated fats do. They can be toxic because they interfere with normal biochemical processes. Trans-fatty Acids have been shown to increase cholesterol, decrease beneficial high density lipoprotein (HDL), interfere with our liver's detoxification system, and interfere with Essential Fatty Acid function (33). The entrée recipes in this book offer a sauté base in olive oil and all of Kitchen Wisdom's gluten free baking recipes use butter.

- Butter produces a soft and chewy crumb (internal texture).

- Recipes which require room temperature butter, indicate that butter should be left out approximately an hour before use.

- Butter breaks down egg white foam and interferes with the bond of egg white.

- Fats make crusts more tender, the fat in a pie shell contributes to the shell's flaky texture.

• Fats help incorporate air into the batter during mixing. The air helps create the volume of a baked good.

• The "moist" in a baked good is most often attributed to the amount of butter, oil or fat used.

• Solid fats like butter when creamed with sugar, create an aerated structure.

Creamed Butter & Sugar: Butter and sugar creamed together create small air pockets. These tiny air pockets form from the crystals of sugar combining with the fat; a finer texture is accomplished when shortening and sugar are creamed together in a baking recipe. The air pockets create an aerated structure. Creaming butter and sugar is a base for some baking, like cookies (biscotti).

Sugar

Sugar raises, delays and controls the temperature in which the batter goes from fluid to solid, which allows the leavening agent to produce the maximum amount of carbon dioxide. Most obviously, it provides sweetness to a baked good.

• Sugar blends and balances flavor components. It potentiates (harmonizes) the flavors.

• It helps stabilize protein bonds, which has a tenderizing or softening effect on proteins.

- Increased sugar increases crispness of gluten free cookies. Temperature and agitation (degree to which it is mixed) produces different crystalline sizes and textures.

- In a solution, sugar has the effect of lowering the freezing point and raising the boiling point of a solution (such as in ice cream – sugar has the ability to slow the freezing process).

- *Heating Sugar*: Caramelization happens when sugar is heated to a sufficiently high temperature. The high temperature causes it to decompose or caramelize. Browning is a reaction in which color is produced when sugars and protein interact in complex ways. The browning is known as a maillard reaction.

- *Concerning yeast*: sugar is consumed by yeast cells in a natural process called fermentation (this is why some people don't set aside just warm water and yeast to rise; they add a pinch of sugar and set it aside to rise).

Leavens & The Process of Leavening

A leavening agent is a substance which releases bubbles of carbon dioxide gas into a batter or dough. The bubbles of carbon dioxide create pockets which hold in the gas and provide shape for the baked good. When a batter or dough is heated, fermented, or has moisture added to it, leaven expands the gas previously created in the recipe, which provides for a light airy texture and contributes to final color.(34) This process allows the baked good to rise.

Leaven lightens and softens the finished baked good. If leavened batter is over mixed or not baked immediately, the gas will escape, leaving the baked good with poor texture and low or dense volume. The leavening agent selected depends upon the balance and type of other ingredients in the recipe.

Baking Powder: Baking Powder is a chemical leaven and is a mixture of acidic salts which lighten and raise baked goods. Baking Powder releases carbon dioxide into the batter causing wet bubbles to pop up and expand in the mixture. The batter expands again when placed in the oven. This action is called "double acting" and is what creates a light and airy baked good. All of my recipes call for double acting baking powder. Since gluten free flours are "weak" flours (lacking in ability to create protein bonds which rise on their own like wheat) expired baking powder is useless and very noticeable in gluten free baking.

Baking Soda (also called sodium bicarbonate): Baking soda is a chemical leaven which helps a baked good rise. Used in baking, it is an alkaline which reacts with acidic ingredients in the recipe to release carbon dioxide (which appear as bubbles or a bubbling action.) Acidic ingredients include: cream of tartar, yogurt, citrus, buttermilk, cocoa, molasses and vinegar (35). If using an acidic ingredient in baking, you will need to add baking soda. Using too much can result in a soapy taste.

Cream of Tartar: An acidic salt, created during wine making. Often it is one of the acidic salts in Baking Powder.

Salt (also called sodium):

- In leavening, *salt* regulates fermentation

- Salt slows down the chemical reactions in batter or dough.

- Makes dough a little stronger and tighter.

- Salt absorbs water and traps moisture from the air into the finished product during storage.

- Salt adds flavor and increases the flavor of other ingredients, such as butter and flour; it can tone down sweetness or bitterness in baked good.

- The American Heart Association recommends we all return to their 2005 Dietary Guidelines of 1500 mg of sodium per day, citing that the current recommendation of 2300 mg per day is too high (36).

Vinegar: As a leavener, vinegar helps to increase volume, puffiness and height; it must be used with an additional leavener like baking soda or baking powder.

Yeast: A micro-organism which thrives in an acidic environment and responsible for giving flours rise.   Gluten rich and gluten free breads rely enormously on yeast for height and structure.

Natural Gum - What is it?

Light airy structure and tender crumb are all possible with the use of natural gum. Gluten free baking requires additional binding to assist the action of leavening with baking powder or baking soda. Natural Gums (such as Guar, Xanthan or Locust Bean) are additives which assist gluten free batter during baking by holding carbon dioxide gas; this increases viscosity (resistance of fluid to flow.) The gums mimic gluten by retaining the gas. Natural gum provides elasticity, height and spring to baked goods. They also keep the baked item from being too crumbly. Gums in the food industry are used as thickening agents, emulsifying agents and stabilizers.

Guar Gum: comes from the cluster beans (or seeds) of the guar plant (a legume) which are processed into flour. It must be used in combination with a traditional leavener (baking powder and/or baking soda) and is active at any temperature.

• Guar is a natural food thickener, emulsifier, stabilizer, binder and gelling agent. It is active at any temperature.

• Provides elasticity, height and stretch to baked goods when combined with baking powder or baking soda.

• Can be used as a volume for volume exchange for Xanthan gum.

• Used in many prepackaged puddings, canned sauces and ice cream in the American market.

• Has the ability to bind with water molecules and prevent the formation of crystals, it therefore can bind ingredients and help create a creamy texture. It is often used in ice cream for this purpose.

• It is a water soluble fiber (it is capable of being dissolved in hot or cold water) and can function as a laxative in therapeutic dosage or for those who are sensitive to it.

Locust Bean Gum: Extracted from the seeds of the carob pod. Must be used in combination with a traditional leavener (baking powder and/or baking soda.)

• Is a thickener and a gelling agent.

• Provides elasticity, height and springiness to baked goods as a leavener, must be used in combination with another leavener (baking powder and or baking soda.)

Xanthan Gum: A thickener and stabilizer generally derived from corn. Xanthan Gum must be used in combination with a traditional leavener (baking powder and/or baking soda) and is active at any temperature.

• Provides elasticity, height and springy-ness to baked goods as a leavener.

• It gives a recipe stretching or elasticity and keeps baked item from being too crumbly.

• It is a manufactured fermented food product, its initial chemical base is derived from corn. Some people have xanthan gum sensitivity, which can create inflammation in people who suffer with irritable bowel syndrome.

Leaven & Natural Gum Formula for Gluten Free Baking

When starting out, use the following *guideline* for a batch of batter. In time you will see what works best for your recipes:

Assume 2 cups of batter:

Cakes   =   2 teaspoons Baking Powder to 1 teaspoon Natural Gum

Cookies =   1 teaspoon Baking Powder   to ½ teaspoon Natural Gum

Create Your Own Culinary Cultural Evolution

Or just convert your favorite baking recipes! I offer you an approach to begin to build your own gluten free recipes. I recommend you begin your gluten free baking journey by first perfecting existing recipes that interest you. Make them according to how the author has instructed. Pay close attention to each flour you use: smell it, observe how much is used, and observe the final flavor as well as final texture. You will find you do not agree with every author and every recipe. This is where I recommend you begin to change things up. Use different flour in a volume for volume exchange. Perhaps add or reduce moisture from a recipe.

Use your senses to learn and observe how the ingredients interact. If you were once able to mix up and rearrange baking recipes with wheat (like muffins, cookies, cakes, etc.) you will easily learn to transform recipes to gluten free. If you are an intermediate cook or baker who likes to create recipes, you can learn to convert recipes to gluten free. If you are new to cooking or baking, be patient with yourself. Above all, never sacrifice flavor just to have something look like a gluten rich item! Gluten free flours look different and therefore yield different hues of color in final baked goods. Gluten free baked goods need not be dry - in fact dry and crumbly are unnecessary.

The following are some highlights of the previous information for you to consider when transforming a gluten rich recipe to gluten free.

Carbohydrates provide bulk to a baked good and use a volume to volume exchange (for example: 1 cup wheat flour=1 cup gluten free flour or gluten free flour combination).

Moisture plays an important function in all baked goods (both savory and sweet); Knowing how to manipulate moisture is pinnacle to transforming recipes. Some wonderful moisture additions milks (nut, seed, rice and dairy); mayonnaise (soy or egg based); cream cheese and other soft spreadable cheeses; tofu; butter; yogurt (dairy or soy); sour cream (soy or milk based); fruit; vegetable and water.

Protein in baked goods provides the foundation for structure, texture and elasticity.

Leaven & Natural Gums together provide elasticity and stretch to baked goods. If over mixed or not baked immediately, the carbon dioxide gas will escape, leaving the baked good with poor texture and low or dense volume. The leavening agent selected depends upon the balance and type of other ingredients in the recipe.

One need not worry about how the baked good will rise, or even how the ingredients work together when baking with wheat. In my opinion, not needing to understand how gluten rich baking works is what made gluten rich baking so easy. *Forget What You Know About Wheat* and don't be afraid to try transforming your favorite recipes! Gluten Free Cooking and Baking can offer a delicious end result which often has bolder flavor than its gluten rich counterpart! Enjoy your own culinary excursion and create your own *Kitchen Wisdom*...Buon Appetito!

Breadcrumb & Coatings

Pangrattato e Rivestimenti

Breadcrumb gluten free

I learned about breadcrumb in the kitchen with my paternal grandmother, Marie Conforti. Extended family is a common tradition in many cultures throughout the world. My grandmother, like so many brides back in her day, moved into a home with her in-laws. My great grandmother Adelina Demari taught her sons and my grandmother how to cook. I was an infant when my Great Grandmother passed away, yet her *Kitchen Wisdom* still extended to me.

Although it took a while to get there, mastering the culinary transformation of gluten rich breadcrumb to gluten free was my turning point. It was the moment I believed I was going to understand my way in a gluten free kitchen.

Previously, I had tried what seemed like every gluten free breadcrumb available on the market and found little satisfaction. One afternoon, while navigating the flour section of my natural food store, I decided to throw caution to the wind! Desperately craving flavor and the correct texture for breadcrumb coating, I decided to forget what I knew about cooking with wheat and truly explore gluten free flours.

I began with gluten free coatings. I learned how to use grains in ways I had never experienced. I experimented with (and now often use) ceci (garbanzo bean/chickpea) flour or sorghum flour for light dusting or dredging. Dredging is a single process, just about any gluten free flour works well.   The combinations and flavors for gluten free breadcrumb and coatings are as limitless as one's flavor imagination.

The greatest foundation in many coating recipes is the *"double dip"* method. *Double dip* refers to plunging the food in egg and breadcrumb or gluten free flour twice before cooking. This allows the food to stay juicy and moist, sealed and steaming in a protective coating from the hostility of the cooking oil. As my flavor imagination increased, I experimented and learned to use polenta (coarse corn meal) in combination with ceci flour or masa harina for a thicker coating on a cutlet. Nut and seed meals are also delicious for thicker coatings.

In the following recipes, I have shown you which flour combinations and coatings I prefer. However, I encourage you to develop your own breadcrumb palate. Play around; create your own unique flavoring for a dish. Your family and friends won't be able to figure out how you've done it! To get started, please keep one thing in mind: begin your journey by breaking free from the wheat box. Allow your senses and palate to be your guide.

I searched a long time for gluten free breadcrumbs. Many store bought mixtures are incredibly expensive with little flavor and poor performance. I was at a friend's home for a wine and cheese sort of afternoon. She had kindly purchased rice crackers as chips for me to eat with gluten free dip. I enjoyed the crackers and found them tasty. Suddenly I had a revelation - ground in a food processor the crackers could be used for breadcrumb. What an epiphany! I'm kind of embarrassed it took so long to conjure. Rice crackers come in various flavors, such as sesame. Sesame is my favorite for breadcrumb as it imparts a harmonizing mellow and traditional flavor. Just be sure the label states the rice crackers are gluten free.

Sesame Meal: A quarter cup or more of sesame seed ground in a spice mill and stored in an airtight container in the freezer is always a worthy project. Sesame is a classic player in Italian flavoring, cooking and baking. I use a bit in breadcrumb mixtures as it adds that "what did you put in this?" secret ingredient enticement for your guests.

A Note about the Addition of Grated Cheese in Breadcrumb Mixtures: **Grated cheese** is usually optional. I prefer Locatelli which is a sheep's milk cheese. It is the grating cheese I was raised with and still prefer. We all tend to use what pleases our taste; my mom now prefers Parmigaianno, Regianno or Asiago. Use the grating cheese which you find most appealing. I encourage you to mix and match your own breadcrumb mixture! Always be willing to try other flour combinations, like almonds or walnuts meal.

The following mixtures create a flavorful course dry breadcrumb:

"Breadcrumb" Mixture A:

½ cup gluten free Masa Harina flour

¼ cup gluten free Polenta meal (coarse)

2 tablespoon Grated Cheese

¼ teaspoon Garlic granules or powder

¼ teaspoon Onion granules or powder

¼ teaspoon salt

Optional 1 tablespoon grated cheese (Locatelli, Asiago, etc.)

"Breadcrumb" Mixture B:

½ cup gluten free Sesame Rice Crackers ground fine

¼ cup Sesame meal

¼ teaspoon Garlic granules or powder

¼ teaspoon Onion granules or powder

¼ teaspoon Salt

Optional 1 tablespoon grated cheese (Locatelli, Asiago, etc.)

Stuffed Artichokes gluten free

Carciofi Ripieni

This special recipe creates a melt in your mouth texture and is absolutely delicious. Cook artichokes in a Pressure Cooker or Dutch oven on the stovetop for at least an hour and a half. Artichokes are part of the thistle family. Just cut off the top, use a melon baller to scoop out the inner seed shoots (the furry internal growth which sits atop the heart of the choke) peel the hard and cracked outer leaves, stuff and then in the pan they go! The heat and steam from the broth does the rest of the work.

Yields 4 Artichokes

4 Globe Artichokes

1 Lemon

32 ounces Chicken Broth (vegetable broth or water can be used instead)

Olive Oil

Breadcrumb Mixture:

3 large finely chopped Garlic cloves

2 teaspoons of Lemon Zest

¾ cup finely ground gluten free Rice Cracker meal

¼ cup finely grated hard Italian cheese

¼ teaspoon onion powder

½ teaspoon dried parsley

Crushed Red Pepper to taste

Pinch of Salt

¼ cup + 2 tablespoons Olive Oil

1 teaspoon Lemon juice

To keep the artichokes from turning black and spotty, place water in a bowl ample enough to accommodate artichokes during prep. Halve the lemon and squeeze it into water bowl, place half of the lemon in bowl.

In a separate bowl combine the breadcrumb mixture, set aside.

Prep the Artichoke: Take the artichoke and chop off the top ½ - ¾ inch. Then chop off the stem. Remove the really dry and cracked outer leaves. Use your fingers to loosen the internal sides of the choke. *Scoop out the inner flower bud*: Use a melon baller to remove the inner hair which sits atop the center (or the heart) of the artichoke. Place the choke in the bowl of water with the lemon.

After the artichokes are hollowed out, hold each one upside down and gently shake excess water from them. Use a tablespoon, stuff each with breadcrumb mixture. Place stuffed artichokes inside of pressure cooker insert or at bottom of a 2 or 3 quart Dutch oven. Squeeze a bit of remaining lemon juice from fresh lemon over stuffed artichokes. Drizzle a bit of olive oil over each artichoke. Pour the broth into Pressure Cooker or Dutch oven.

Place lid atop pot, be sure it is sealed. Begin by cooking on medium high for about 20 minutes. Steam and rolling simmer noise will be heard, reduce heat to low and cook for another hour and a half. Turn off heat, do not remove lid. Allow artichokes to sit in lidded pot for at least another 20 minutes before serving. Be sure to spoon additional broth over stuffed artichoke for serving.

Stuffed Mushrooms gluten free

I love Stuffed Mushrooms. It was one of the first recipes I learned to prepare and bake when I was around the age of ten. I remember being around 12 when my mom received a food processor; it was then that I recall making my first recipe alteration. After separating the stems from the caps, I trim the ends of the stems and place them in the food processor with a clove or more of garlic. The rest of the recipe can be prepared in a bowl using a fork, the same way my grandmother, Marie Conforti, taught me. These mushrooms are great straight from the oven, room temperature or as leftovers cut up in salad. If you have additional filling left over, spread it on a cookie sheet and bake until it becomes crispy crumbles. Cool completely, serve on salad. The crumbly mixture can be stored in a covered jar in fridge for a couple of days.

8 ounces Baby Bella mushrooms, caps only – stems removed

2 cloves Garlic, super finely chopped

¼ cup gluten free Rice Cracker Crumbs-medium fine ground

½ teaspoon Parsley (dried)

1 ½ tablespoons Olive Oil

3 tablespoons Water (for baking)

2 teaspoons Hard Italian Grating Cheese

Pinch Salt

(Optional) Crushed Red Pepper to taste

Pre-heat the oven to 350 degrees. Use an oven safe baking dish with at least 2" sides. Drizzle inside of dish with 1-2 teaspoons of olive oil, under the surface area of where the mushrooms will sit. Separate the mushroom caps from the stems, pat dirt off of the mushrooms with a paper towel. Leave caps on side.

Stuffed Mushrooms gluten free

Funghi Ripieni senza glutine

Trim the shoots (stems) by slicing off the bottom end - about 1/8" of the shoot. Gently pluck the stems away from the caps. Place the trimmed shoots with the garlic in the food processor. All that is necessary are a few pulses; enough to break up the stems and garlic, creating a loose mash. Add the mushroom stem & garlic mixture to breadcrumb mixture. Toss with fork until well combined.

Fill caps by the teaspoon full. Hold cap with one hand and gently tilt cap while filling cap with teaspoon of mixture with other hand. Line stuffed mushrooms about 1 – 1 ½ inches apart in baking pan. Crumble ¾ teaspoon grated cheeses in between your fingers and loosely apply just a little to the top of each mushroom.

Drizzle 3 Tablespoons of water along the side of the baking dish – NOT on the mushrooms themselves. Use a spoon to drizzle the remaining olive over the stuffed mushrooms.

Place in center of pre-heated oven. Cover loosely and bake for 20 minutes, then remove cover and continue to bake for 10 additional minutes.

Allow mushrooms to cool a bit before serving.

Mozzarella Sticks gluten free

I have to admit, I just love these, despite their decadence! I often serve appetizers for gatherings with friends. I really missed these for a long time during those dark first years of gluten free eating and am excited to share this wonderful creation.

Yields approximately 18

Breadcrumb Mixture:

1 cup ground gluten free Sesame Cracker Crumbs

½ teaspoon granulated Garlic

½ teaspoon granulated Onion

1 teaspoon Parsley Flakes

1 tablespoon hard Italian Grated Cheese

¼ teaspoon Salt

(optional) Crushed Red Pepper Flakes to taste

½ pound Mozzarella cheese, sliced as described below.

Combine breadcrumb mixture in a shallow bowl. Place aside.

To Prepare Mozzarella Cheese: ½ pound cold mozzarella (1/2 conventional supermarket brick.) Slice ½" thick pieces, then slice each again (long way), then slice again in center – this creates 4 sticks per ½" slice. Return cheese to plate and place in fridge until ready to cook them.

In a shallow bowl beat 2 eggs, place aside. Place paper towel on top of a large serving plate, place aside.

Mozzarella Sticks gluten free

Frito di Mozzarella senza glutine

Place one mozzarella in the egg, using your fingers, coat cheese completely. Then dip in breadcrumb mixture – be sure to coat all sides.

Repeat and double dip. Dip in egg and then again in breadcrumb. The uncooked cheese sticks can be lined up directly on a fresh plate.

Place a 12-14" fry pan on flame and warm to medium high. Pour enough olive oil to coat pan (about 3 Tablespoons), allow to warm thoroughly. (Don't use the highest end olive oil for frying.) If the oil smokes, it is too high and should be discarded.

Once the oil is heated, add the dipped cheese sticks. Watch for too much melt. They only take about 30 seconds to cook, flip, cook 30 seconds on the other side, and remove to plate lined with paper towel.

How to know oil is ready to fry: Old school approach - no fancy thermometers will be used - just the end of a wooden spoon. Once oil has been in pan 40 – 60 seconds on medium high, it will move in a much more fluid manner. Once this happens begin testing the oil by placing the handle end of a wooden spoon in the oil. When very small bubbles begin to form at the base of the handle, the oil is ready!

Spinach Fritters gluten free

Crunchy on the outside, smooth and yummy on the inside –serve these delicious fritters with salad to make a meal.

Yields approximately 13 – 2" fritters

Spinach Mixture:

2 Garlic cloves minced or ½ teaspoon garlic granules

1 cup chopped thawed frozen Spinach

2 Eggs, beaten

3-4 tablespoons Olive Oil

Breadcrumb Mixture:

3/4 cup gluten free Sesame Rice Crackers ground fine

¼ cup Grated Cheese (Locatelli, Asiago, Parmesan, etc.)

¼ teaspoon Garlic granules

¼ teaspoon Onion granules

¼ teaspoon Salt

(Optional) crushed Red Pepper

Spinach Fritter Coating:

Place ¼ cup Sesame Rice Crackers processed to fine texture in food processor, then place in a shallow bowl and set aside. (This is an excellent opportunity to use some ground Sesame Meal in the breadcrumb mixture to increase flavor and protein.)

Spinach Fritters gluten free

Frittelle di Spinaci senza glutine

Prepare Breadcrumb Mixture: ¾ cup Sesame Rice Crackers ground fine, grated cheese, garlic granules, onion granules, salt. Place aside.

Place final ¼ cup cracker meal in a shallow bowl. Place aside.

Prepare the Spinach: Press the spinach to remove excess liquid. Chop the spinach and mix in ½ teaspoon garlic granules. Beat 2 eggs and mix them into the spinach.   Mix in Breadcrumb mixture. Combine thoroughly.   The final mixture should feel damp NOT wet. If too wet, add more 'breadcrumb'.

Make the Fritters: Using your hands, pluck 2 inch dollop, place in reserved cracker meal in shallow bowl. Press lightly with fingers, flip and press slightly with fingers again and form into a flattish round.

Warm fry pan on medium high heat with olive oil enough to coat pan by 1/8"-1/4". When oil is hot, place fritters into oil (leave about an inch or more between fritters in pan during cooking). Cook 6 minutes, flip with spatula, flatten with back of spatula once flipped. Cook on opposite side 6 minutes. Watch that oil does not smoke. When cooked, place cooked fritters on plate lined with paper towel to cool.

Bake instead of Fry: Pre-heat oven to 375 degrees.   These can also be formed and placed on a parchment lined cookie sheet. Bake 25 minutes, flip 14 minutes into baking. Serve warm or at room temperature.

Sausage & Spinach Fritters gluten free

Salsiccia e Spinaci Fritelle senza glutine

Tasty as an appetizer or a side dish! Everyone enjoys these flavors, great for entertaining!

Yields approximately 10 – 2" fritters

¾ pound gluten free Sausage, casings removed
2 Garlic cloves, finely chopped
1 ½cups chopped cooked Spinach
2 Eggs, beaten
3-4 tablespoons Olive Oil

Breadcrumb Mixture:
1 cup gluten free Sesame Rice Crackers ground fine
¼ cup Grated Cheese
¼ teaspoon Garlic granules
¼ teaspoon Onion granules
¼ teaspoon Salt
Optional crushed Red Pepper
3/4 cup Sesame Rice Crackers, ground fine

Remove the casings of the sausage. Finely chop the garlic. Crumble the meat into a dry medium hot frying pan, separate meat as it cooks. Create small pellet size bits of pork. When the meat just begins to brown, add finely chopped garlic and continue to cook until the meat if fully browned. Remove sausage to shallow bowl or plate and leave aside.

Prepare the Spinach: Chop cooked spinach. I often use leftover spinach. When using frozen, be sure it is fully thawed, pressed and chopped.

Prepare Breadcrumb Mixture for fritter: Combine the ground sesame rice crackers, grated cheese, garlic granules, onion granules, and salt. Set aside.

Place ¼ cup breadcrumb in a shallow bowl and place aside for final dredging before fritter goes into pan.

Beat eggs, fold eggs into chopped spinach, add sausage to spinach egg mixture. Working with your hands, gradually add breadcrumb to the mixture. The final mixture should feel damp NOT wet. If too wet, add more breadcrumb.

Make the Fritters: Pull 2 inches of mixture and flatten with palms of hands. Then dredge formed fritter in breadcrumb mixture. Place on plate on side until you have enough fritters to fill fry pan, or until you have no more mixture.

Warm fry pan on medium high heat with 2 tablespoons of olive oil; when oil is hot, use a tablespoon to dollop 2 inch diameter fritters in pan (leave about an inch or more between fritters in pan during cooking).

Cook 7 minutes, flip with spatula, flatten with back of spatula once flipped. Cook on opposite side 5 minutes.   Place cooked fritters on plate lined with paper towel to cool. Enjoy!

Broccoli Fritters gluten free

These have so much flavor, everyone will enjoy! The batter can sit prepared in refrigerator for a few hours before making. They re-heat very well.

Yields approximately 13 – 2" fritters

Broccoli Mixture:

½ teaspoon Garlic granules

16 ounce thawed (frozen) Broccoli spears, thoroughly drained of liquid

1 cup shredded provolone cheese (cheddar is delicious as well)

1 Eggs white

¾ cup gluten free Sesame Rice Crackers ground fine

¼ cup Grated Cheese

¼ teaspoon Garlic granules

¼ teaspoon Onion granules

¼ teaspoon Salt

Optional crushed Red Pepper

Olive Oil enough to coat bottom of fry pan by 1/8 – ¼ inch

Fritter Coating: 1/3 cup Sesame Rice Crackers to fine texture in food processor. (This is an excellent opportunity to use some ground Sesame Meal in the breadcrumb mixture to increase flavor and protein.)

Prepare Breadcrumb Mixture: 2/3 cup Sesame Rice Crackers finely ground, grated cheese, garlic granules, onion granules, salt. Place aside.

Place final 1/3 cup finely ground rice cracker meal in a shallow bowl for dredging fritters just before cooking. Place aside.

Broccoli Fritters   gluten free

Frittelle di Broccoli senza glutine

Prepare the Broccoli: Defrost, chop finely or process in food processor. Squeeze out excess liquid. Using hands or large fork, combine in shredded cheese and egg white. Then add reserved breadcrumb mixture. Thoroughly combine with hands. The final mixture should feel damp NOT wet. If too wet, add more breadcrumb.

Make the Fritters: Using your hands, pluck 2 inch dollop, place in cracker meal in shallow bowl. Press lightly with fingers, flip and press slightly with fingers again and form into a flattish round 2 inches in diameter.

Warm fry pan on medium high heat with 2 tablespoons of olive oil; when oil is hot, use a tablespoon to dollop 2 inch diameter fritters in pan (leave about an inch or more between fritters in pan during cooking).

Cook 6 minutes, flip with spatula, flatten with back of spatula once flipped. Cook on opposite side 6 minutes.   Place cooked fritters on plate lined with paper towel to cool.

Meatballs gluten free

Many years ago a friend of mine from Calabria showed me how she makes her meatballs. She is somewhat famous for her recipe with family and friends. Her secret to a moist meatball is 3 eggs per pound of chopped meat. Also, this is an interesting recipe because they cook in the sauce and do not need to be pre-cooked. I use the Sunday Tomato Sauce recipe from page 105.

Yields approximately 8 – 4 inch meatballs

1 pound lean ground Beef

3 whole Eggs

½ cup Grated hard Italian Cheese

1 ¼ cups finely ground gluten free Rice Cracker crumbs

You will need a large platter, plate or cookie sheet to place the meatballs on when done assembly. Place the meat in a large bowl. Use your hands to add and work the eggs into the meat. Still using your hands, sprinkle the grated cheese and thoroughly combine into the meat. Finally, add the rice cracker crumbs. Continue to work all of the ingredients together until completely combined.

Pluck 4.5"-5" of meatball mixture with your hand, roll between hands to create a ball. Place on platter. Repeat until all of the mixture has been used. They can be placed aside at this time. They store very well covered with plastic wrap in the fridge for a few hours. Or just move forward and cook them.   Bring tomato sauce to a rolling simmer. Place meatballs, one a time, in the sauce. Be sure they are each covered with sauce. Cook in this manner for

30 minutes. To stir sauce, you will need to be careful not to break the meatballs. As they cook, they become sturdier. Enjoy!

Dredging and Flour Coatings gluten free

Dredging any type of cutlet in flour and then pan frying is a delicious way of using any of the following flour blends. Flour coatings work well for thin cutlet cuts of meat, poultry or vegetables. For any cutlet dredged in flour, substituting the flour for gluten free flour is all that is necessary. But what flour? Ceci flour will impart a full bottom flavor, almost nutty. Sesame flour will impart a billowy – secret unknown ingredient – sort of flavor. Masa Harina (finely ground corn) flour imparts a sweet flavor which catches the top of palate. Almond flour imparts a rich flavor, as does chestnut flour. Sorghum most closely resembles the flavor of wheat, but can be a bit overpowering and dry – it is best used in moderation for dredging.

Mixture A:

¾ cup gluten free Masa Harina

¼ teaspoon Salt

¼ teaspoon Garlic Granules

¼ teaspoon Onion Granules

Mixture B:

½ cup gluten free Cici (Garbanzo Bean/Chickpea) Flour

¼ cup Sesame Meal

¼ teaspoon Salt

¼ teaspoon Garlic Granules

¼ teaspoon Onion Granules

Breaded Chicken Cutlets gluten free

I grew up with these cooked in breadcrumb, I make them coated in seasoned flour. They are delicious hot, or at room temperature. Leftover cutlets are fantastic in a salad the next day. Pound the chicken thin before coating. The chicken in this recipe sits in a thick coating, so the double dip method is best employed here.

1 pound Chicken cutlets cleaned and pounded thin

2 whole Eggs, beaten

3-4 tablespoons Extra Virgin Olive Oil

Breadcrumb Mixture:

¾ cup gluten free Cici (Garbanzo Bean/Chickpea) Flour

¼ teaspoon Salt

¼ teaspoon granulated Garlic

¼ teaspoon granulated Onion

1/8 teaspoon Salt

2 Eggs, beaten

Place the flour, salt and granulated garlic in a shallow bowl. Mix thoroughly with fork. In another shallow bowl, vigorously beat the eggs.

   Create an assembly line: chicken, gluten free flour mixture, egg.

   Also line a plate or cookie sheet with paper towel.

   The chicken cutlets should be around 3/8" thick.

Breaded Chicken Cutlets gluten free

Cotoletta di Pollo Impanata senza glutine

Dredge and double dip both sides of each cutlet in flour, then egg, then flour again. To dredge thoroughly, use fork and shift and swirl cutlet around the inside of the flour bowl. Lightly and evenly coat each side of the cutlet with flour. Dredge in egg, return to the flour bowl for another swirl. Place cutlet on fresh plate to await cooking.

Warm fry pan to medium high, add 1 tablespoon of oil to pan, allow to heat all of the way through. An even coating of oil lining the pan is all that is necessary.

Add cutlets to the pan, allowing room between them so the air circulation can help them cook properly.

Cook approximately 5 minutes on one side, then about 3-4 minutes on the other. When the cutlet is ready to be flipped, the poultry will begin to whiten at all ends and sweat in its center. Also, bubbles will form on the sides of the cutlets which will be strong and consistent. Add additional oil to pan as necessary. Drizzle between the cutlets when pan gets too dry.

Remove cutlets to plate covered with paper towel.

Serve immediately or at room temperature.

Baked Eggplant with Salame & Mozzarella gluten free

Melanzane al Forno con Salame e Mozarella senza glutine

So tasty! Not a common dish, but once you share it prepare to be asked to make it again. The eggplant is dredged in Ceci flour then quickly fried in olive oil. If beans are difficult for you to digest use sorghum flour. The eggplant must be sliced very thin for full flavor. The meat must be super thin as well, be sure to use salame which is labeled gluten free. This dish is outstanding with Prosciutto, whichever pork you choose do not compromiser flavor by purchasing an inferior brand.

2 pounds Eggplant, sliced thin

¼ cup gluten free Cici (Garbanzo/Chickpea) Flour

Olive Oil

¼ pound thinly sliced good quality gluten free Genoa Salame or Prosciutto

1 pound shredded Mozzarella cheese

Press the Eggplant: Remove Bitters from the Eggplant, if you use a standard American Globe Eggplant, this step is absolutely necessary. Slice eggplant into 1/8 inch thick rounds. Place large colander in sink. Line eggplant in colander in this way: a few eggplant at the bottom, lightly salt, a few more, lightly salt – until you have used up all the eggplant. Place a plate with weight at the top and allow eggplant's bitters to press out. Leave for an hour or more. Remove dish, use paper towel to soak

Baked Eggplant with Salame & Mozzarella gluten free

Melanzane al Forno con Salame e Mozarella senza glutine

brownish liquid (the bitters) from flesh. Place all flat on paper towel and put aside until ready to fry.

Dredge the Eggplant: Place ceci (chickpea) flour in a shallow bowl. Dredge the eggplant through the flour on both sides, shake off excess.

Fry the Eggplant: add about 2 teaspoons of olive oil to a well heated fry pan. Use little oil, the eggplant soak up oil like a sponge. Manage heat and have them cook with as little additional oil as possible. Don't let oil smoke. Cook eggplant slices no more than 2-3 minutes on each side on medium heat. Remove to paper towel to soak up any residual oil. Eggplant can cool to room temperature. At this point, you can store eggplant in sealed container for a day or two.

Pre-heat the oven to 325 degrees. Prepare an 8" x 10" baking dish with a thin coating of olive oil. Place aside. Place a layer of eggplant at the bottom of the dish. Follow by a single layer of salame. Put a thin layer of shredded mozzarella across the salame. Add another layer of eggplant and repeat the layers until you reach the end of available eggplant. After placing the final layer of eggplant, top with mozzarella cheese. Bake uncovered 35 minutes until bubbling at edges. Remove from oven, allow to set at least 15 minutes before cutting to plate.

Preparing an Eggplant to cook: Wash the eggplant and hold it on its side, slice off the bottom about a half an inch from the lower button. Slice rounds, thin - about a 1/8 – ¼ of an inch in thickness. Lay each slice in a colander large enough to accommodate all of the eggplant, lightly salt each slice. Stack in a staggered manner around the colander. The salt draws the bitters out of the vegetables. Place a flat bowl or plate in the colander, on top of the eggplant slices. If the eggplant is small and slender it will not need to be weighted.   If using an *American Globe* eggplant: Place a weight (I use flat river rocks) in the plate atop the eggplant. Locate a plate or shallow bowl which will fit under the colander. Allow to sit like this for one hour. Remove plate with weight. Use a paper towel to pat off the dark liquid (bitters) from each slice and pat dry. Transfer eggplant to a plate. This process allows the eggplant to be super sweet when cooked.

Choosing an Eggplant: Choose an eggplant which is slender and has a sturdy sound when lightly knocked with your knuckles. The color should be even and unblemished. The eggplant should not have any squishy areas.

Types of Eggplant: Eggplant is a nightshade. It grows in many types of climates. Technically classified as a berry, the seeds are edible, but contain a bitter taste. Persons who are sensitive to it may experience itchiness in the mouth, or slight stomach upset with or without mild headache after ingesting.

Chinese and Japanese Eggplants are long and slender and their colors are varying degrees of purple and violet. *Indian Eggplant*: are round and have a light color. They are very sweet. *Italian Eggplant*: are generally smaller and more slender than the American Globe Eggplant, but bear a very similar shape. *American Globe Eggplant*: These tend to be the most bitter of all eggplants. The bitters need to be pressed out of them, the others don't.

Tender Pork Cutlets with Tomatoes gluten free

This dish is really packed with flavor! The pork cutlets in this recipe are pounded super thin and very lightly dredged in flour. The flour of the dredge provides bulk and body as a base for the delicious and almost tangy sauce the pork cooks in.   I use ceci flour (garbanzo bean/chickpea) but other gluten free flours work really well for dredging. The key is to not use a starch (like potato starch) because it will clump while cooking and won't disperse properly in the heated liquid. The taste of this recipe makes people say "what is that extra ingredient you used? It is delicious but I can't place it..." I am not joking; this is

gluten free application where the gluten free flavors can be so enticing that they out flavor wheat.

Yields approximately 6 cutlets

1 pound thin boneless Pork cutlets (loin or even center cut can be used), pounded super thin

3 tablespoons gluten free Ceci (Garbanzo Bean/Chickpea) Flour

1 medium large Onion

2 Garlic cloves

1 cup chopped tomatoes with liquid (fresh or canned)

1 cup Chicken Broth

2 tablespoons Olive Oil

Pound the cutlets super thin: Wash and pat dry the pork. Pound the pork cutlets to super thin. Place pork between cutting board and plastic wrap. Use a meat mallet to pound cutlets through plastic wrap. Begin at the center and pound outward until ultimately reaching the ends. Put thin cutlets on plate, place covered in fridge until ready to dredge and cook.

Slice onions into thin ringlets. Make thin slices of the garlic. Chop tomatoes if using fresh, or just use one cup of canned tomatoes.

In a heavy bottomed fry or sauté pan, add about 2 teaspoons of olive oil (just enough to coat pan). Once warm, add onions and sauté for a few minutes. Then add the garlic and sprinkle with salt. Cook for a bit, reduce heat to low, cover slightly and allow vegetables to completely wilt, cooking about 10 minutes. Remove onions and garlic to a small bowl and place aside.

Place flour in shallow bowl. Reheat pan to medium high, add about a tablespoon of olive oil. Dredge the cutlets on each side in flour and then add to pan. Be sure there is ample room between cutlets; you may have to make a few batches. Cook cutlets about 2 minutes or less on each side. Just enough to turn outer skin white and dredged coating begins to brown. Remove from pan and place on plate, leave aside.

Once all of the cutlets are pre-cooked and the pan is emptied of meat, place pan back medium heat. Scrape bits of meat with spoon, add just a bit more olive oil to the pan, followed by the tomatoes, cook a few moments and then add the reserved cooked onions and garlic. Pour the chicken broth into the pan, stir, lower heat and cook for a couple of minutes. Return the cutlets to the pan. Make sure cutlets are covered in liquid, place lid on pan slightly ajar. Cook 15 minutes on medium low heat, flip cutlets and cook an additional 15 minutes. The gluten free flour coating on the cutlets will provide bulk to the liquid and harmonizes to make a delectable sauce.   Serve with some of the liquid and vegetables ladled on top.

Eggplant Rollatini gluten free

Eggplant Rollatini are delicious as a meal with salad. They re-heat very well and are a great leftover lunch for a busy workweek. I grew up making a ricotta mixture with egg, but I learned from Italian American friend's families the filling is equally as delicious without the eggs. Once rollatini are done, allow dish to sit and cool down for at least 20 minutes. This allows the ricotta mixture to set within the eggplant. I use the Sunday Tomato Sauce recipe on page 105 to go with the eggplant.

Yields 6

2 long slender Asian Eggplants, or 1 small American Globe Eggplant

2-3 tablespoons Ceci (Chickpea/Garbanzo) Bean Flour

¼ cup Olive Oil for frying

1 cup Ricotta

6 ounces shredded Mozzarella

2 tablespoons grated cheese (Locatelli, etc.)

1 ½ cups Tomato Sauce

Press the Eggplant (Remove Bitters from the Eggplant): If you use a small Asian eggplant - this step is unnecessary. If you use a standard American Globe Eggplant, this step is absolutely necessary. Slice eggplant to ¼ of an inch thickness. Place large colander in sink. Line eggplant in colander in this way: a few at the bottom,

Eggplant Rollatini gluten free

Involtini di Melanzine senza glutine

lightly salt, a few more, lightly salt – until you have used up all the eggplant. Place a plate with weight at the top and allow eggplant's bitters to press out. Leave for an hour or more. Remove plate with weight and use paper towel to soak up brownish liquid (bitters). Place eggplant slices on paper towel and set aside until ready to fry.

Prepare the Eggplant to Fry: Place 3 tablespoons of cici (chickpea) flour in a shallow bowl. One slice of eggplant at a time, dredge eggplant slice through the flour on both sides, shake off excess, place in prepared hot fry pan.

Fry the Eggplant: add 1 tablespoon of olive oil to a well heated fry pan. Use little oil, the eggplant soak up oil like a sponge. Manage heat and have them cook with as little additional oil as possible. Don't let oil get hot enough to smoke. Cook eggplant slices no more than 2-3 minutes on each side on medium heat. Remove to paper towel to soak up any residual oil. Eggplant can cool to room temperature, set aside. At this point, you can store eggplant in sealed container for a day or two if you would like to prepare the rollatini later.

Preheat oven to 350 degrees. Ladle a small amount of tomato sauce to completely cover bottom of baking dish.

Ricotta Mixture: Add ricotta, grated cheese and 3.5 ounces of the mozzarella in a bowl and mix with spoon until well combined.

Create the Rollatini: lay cooled fried eggplant slice flat on plate, place 2 tablespoons of ricotta mixture into center of eggplant, sprinkle top of ricotta mixture with a few shards of shredded mozzarella. Gently roll & slightly tuck the filled eggplant slice, begin from the small end and gently fold into the larger end. Place end upside down in baking dish previously ladled with thin layer of tomato sauce. Repeat these steps until all eggplant slices are tucked into baking dish.

Ladle a few tablespoons of sauce over each rollatini. Sprinkle with remaining shredded mozzarella. Cover and bake in center of oven for 20 minutes. Uncover and bake an additional 10 minutes. Remove from oven and let eggplant rollatini set by allowing it to sit and cool for at least 20 minutes before serving.

Potato Croquettes gluten free

Crocchetti di Patate senza glutine

The holidays always brought delicious annual recipes to our family table. This is such a recipe and is wonderful as an appetizer or a side dish. In Italian cooking, there are many times when foods are dusted in flour or dredged in egg and breadcrumb to create a coating. This recipe is an example of both methods being used. The flour dusting seals the food, followed by a dip in egg and breadcrumbs, which provide a thick coating for the croquette once cooked. This is one of the many recipes I present which require breadcrumbs utilizing rice crackers processed until very fine. They are delicious warm or at room temperature. They store a few days in refrigerator, just warm up for about 15 minutes in a 350 degree heated oven.

Yields approximately 2 dozen

2 pounds Potatoes (Russet)

4 tablespoons Butter

1 ½ cups grated Hard Italian Cheese (like Parmigianna Reggiano)

1 finely mashed Garlic clove

3 tablespoons finely chopped parsley

Salt & Pepper

2 Whole Egg

1 Egg Yolk

Olive Oil for frying

¾ cup gluten free Rice Crackers processed to fine meal

3-4 tablespoons gluten free Ceci (garbanzo bean/chickpea) flour for dusting

Peel and quarter 2 pounds of russet potatoes, bring to a boil in salted water. Reduce water to a rolling simmer on medium high heat. Cook for 20 minutes. Drain immediately; allow to stand in colander for about 5 minutes to drain excess cooking liquid.

Once drained, mash the potatoes. Use whichever tool is comfortable to accomplish this, I use a stand mixer. Mix in butter, then garlic, then parsley, then cheese and salt and pepper to taste. Place mixture aside and cool completely.

Fold in one whole egg and one egg yolk to cooled mixture. Place remaining egg white and whole egg in shallow bowl, whisk and place aside.

Place rice cracker meal in a shallow bowl, set aside. Put 3-4 tablespoons of ceci flour in a shallow bowl, set aside. I line the bowls up in the following order: potato mixture, ceci flour, egg and rice cracker meal.

From the potato mixture, pluck a clump about 1 ½ - 2 inches in girth. Use a swift rolling action: roll into barrel shape. Quickly use your fingers to push/roll the mixture in flour to add a dusting layer to the barrel. Again, using quick motions, dunk in egg – rolling the barrel swiftly toward you; then quickly plunge in breadcrumb bowl – all the while swiftly rolling the barrel toward you. If you are not swift, the egg mixture will be the most challenging. If the potato mixture is too wet, fold in breadcrumb or ceci flour – about one tablespoon at a time until mixture is thick enough to handle.

Warm a fry pan with a thin layer of olive oil to hot (do not allow oil to smoke.) Fry croquettes, turning often in pan, until golden brown. This takes about 4 or 5 minutes. Remove from pan and place on paper towels to drain off excess olive oil.

Soup & Sauce

Zuppa e Salsa

Soup

Many soups available in restaurants begin with a roux for flavor and body. A roux generally uses wheat flour whisked with butter, followed by the slow addition of liquid. As all of the ingredients are added, the roux base thickens as the food cooks. Many pre-packaged soups rely on wheat and gluten containing additives to accomplish the same end. The soups presented use other ingredients which work to thicken the broth and provide body and bulk to the soup. The Broccoli Potato soup relies on potato to accomplish the same end as well as provide a somewhat creamy texture. The Lentil soup can thicken to a stew if scant liquid is added, bean flours also work as delicious bulk as these flours expand in heated liquid. Mombriglio in the chicken soup provide a rice flour base to thicken soup; adding a lot of Mombriglio can also turn a soup into a stew.

Creamy Broccoli Soup Roman Style gluten free

Gluten and Dairy free, this soup is a great example of how to make a rich and thick soup without the use of flour or cream. I boil potato with the broccoli and then use an emulsion blender to puree the vegetables. The result is a smooth, flavorful and satisfying spring soup. Enjoy a heartier meal by serving this Creamy Broccoli Roman Style soup with slices of garlic infused toast.

Yields 4 large bowls of soup

3 Garlic cloves

1 ½ pounds Broccoli

1 pound Russet or Yukon Gold Potatoes

7 ½ cups fresh or boxed Chicken or Vegetable Broth

1 tablespoon Lemon Juice

Salt & Pepper to taste

4 pieces gluten free Bread

Peel potato and cut in chunks. Chop broccoli into small pieces & small florets, place both aside. Bring broth to boil in large pot, add the broccoli, potato & 2 whole peeled garlic cloves. Simmer for 30 minutes. Add lemon juice. Place bread in toaster. Puree vegetables using an emulsion blender or food processor. Blend until smooth, add salt and pepper to taste.

Flavor toast with garlic: Slice remaining garlic clove in half. Rub garlic across entire surface of each slice of toast. Slice toast in triangles or strips and place in soup.

To Serve: Ladle soup into soup bowls. Arrange a pleasing view with toast pieces. Sprinkle with fresh milled black pepper.

Minestrone gluten free

Minestrone is a traditional food which worked its way into American culture; over one hundred ago, Progresso foods began producing canned tomatoes and traditional soups for American mass consumption. I believe this is how minestrone made its way into the cupboards, dinner tables and vernacular of many Americans. A basic farm soup, recipes such as this are common all over Europe and the dining tables of US farming and homesteading families. "Big Soup" as minestrone translates too, is just a soup of lots of things: vegetables, beans and pasta in a stock. Every household cooks it differently. It can also be prepared using different vegetables. The addition of beans gives the soup a bit of bulk and body.

1 ½ cups cooked Kidney Beans (or 16 ounce can drained)

3 cloves finely chopped Garlic

½ cup chopped Onion

1 cup chopped Celery

½ - 1 cup Celery Greens chopped (if possible)

1 cup chopped Carrots

28 ounce can Whole Peeled Tomatoes

32 ounces Beef Stock (homemade or store bought)

2 tablespoons Extra Virgin Olive Oil

½ cup chopped Flat Leaf Italian Parsley

1 small Bay Leaf

(optional) 2 inch Rind of favorite Hard Italian Grating Cheese

Pinch Salt

Milled Black Pepper to taste

Chop and prepare all of the above ingredients. Warm the pan on medium, add 2 tablespoons of olive oil, add garlic and sauté another 30 seconds. Add the Carrots and celery, sauté another minute. Add the zucchini, stir and continue to sauté. Add bay leaf and (optional) half of the celery greens. Gently pass a pinch of salt along all of the vegetables sautéing.

Reduce heat to low, cover the pan and allow vegetables to cook for 3-5 minutes. The salt will help them sweat out their liquids, thereby infusing all of the vegetable with corresponding flavors.

Add the tomatoes next, use your hands, gently squeeze one tomato at a time over the pan. Reserve the liquid from the can to add to the pot later.

Add the pre-cooked or canned red kidney beans.   Raise flame a bit, cover and cook for 3-5 minutes, allows the flavors to begin to marry. Add 4 cups (32 ounces) of beef stock. Add the liquid from the tomatoes. Add 1 cup of water.

Cover and bring to a rolling simmer. Add (optional) rind of locatelli (or other hard Italian grating cheese). Leave at a rolling simmer for 5 minutes. Add ¾ of the parsley leaves and the rest of the celery greens. Place heat to low.

Simmer on low with lid slightly ajar for 40 minutes or longer. Stir every 20 minutes. Serve with small pasta. Gluten Free ditalini are the perfect pairing for this soup, but any small pasta will do. Don't add the pasta directly to the soup, or it will just turn to mush within 15 minutes. Add the pasta to the soup bowl and ladle the soup over it. Serve in Soup bowls with fresh milled pepper and some grated cheese.

Lentil Soup with Sausage gluten free

Zuppa di Lenticchie con Salsiccia senza glutine

This was a signature dish belonging to my paternal grandmother (Marie Conforti.) She taught me this soup when I was quite young. She learned it from my great grandmother (Adelina DeMari Conforti), and taught it to me when I was quite young. This dish uses only two sausages for an entire pot of soup, I suspect the recipe originated this way – utilizing a little of an ingredient and making it stretch for an entire meal is a typical trait of Southern Italian cooking and the tables of family farms across the globe. This soup is more of a stew, perfect on a really cold winter day. If you prefer a soupier base, add an additional 16 ounces of liquid.

Yields 4-6 servings

1/3 cup Onion – chopped

1-4 Garlic cloves finely chopped

1 cup chopped Carrots

1 cup chopped Celery

1 Bay Leaf

2 hot or sweet gluten free Sausage links with fennel (if no sausage with fennel is available, add ½ tsp of fennel when bay leaf is added)

1 ½ cup Green Lentils, washed and picked over (you can use French lentils but will need to adjust cooking time accordingly)

32 ounces Water or chicken broth (I prefer chicken broth)

(Optional) 1 or 2 inch piece rind of Italian Grating cheese

(Optional) Crushed Hot Red Pepper to taste

(Optional) few sprigs of celery greens finely chopped

Sausage Preparation: Purchase lean sausage, remove the casings and any large clumps of fat from the sausage. Prepare crumbles and place aside.

   Clean and chop all of the vegetables. Clean the lentils, first placing them in a colander under running water. Pick them over to remove any debris and place aside.

   Use a large heavy bottomed pot. Place on low flame. When pot is warm, crumble the previously prepped sausage into the pot and increase heat to medium high. Cook until brown on all sides. I try to purchase sausage with as little fat as possible. If there is only a slight coating of grease in the pan, add the onion and garlic (and optional hot pepper) directly to the cooked sausage. If there is too much fat, remove sausage and drain fat to leave only a coating on the surface, and place sausage back in the pot.

Add the onion and sauté for 2 or 3 minutes, then add the garlic and (optional) crushed red pepper, sauté another minute. Once the onions turn translucent add carrot, celery and bay leaf (and fennel if using sausage without fennel), cover with lid slightly ajar and lower flame to medium low. Cook for 5 minutes.

Add the lentils to the pan, stir and sauté all of the ingredients for about a minute. Add 1 cup of liquid (chicken broth, water, vegetable broth – chicken broth is my favorite and the way my grandmother used to make it). Allow to simmer for a minute, stir and scrape up bits of meat from the pan.

Add remainder of liquid (and optional loosely chopped celery leaves). Bring to a rolling simmer, add (optional) grated cheese rind and lower the heat to low. Cover with lid slightly ajar on one edge. Stir every 20 minutes. Cook for 1 ½ -2 hours.

To Serve: Cook some small pasta and serve by placing just a little pasta in the center of a soup bowl. Place lentils over pasta and stir together. The lentils are the center point of the meal, the pasta is just a little added carbohydrate. Serve with fresh grated cheese and fresh cracked black pepper.

Vegetarian Lentil Soup gluten free

Vegetariano Zuppa di Lenticchie senza glutine

There many versions of countryside recipes for lentil soup that use water or vegetable broth. The fennel is the most important ingredient and extends familiar flavor of the better known versions of Italian Lentil Soup which contain sausage.

Yields 4-6 servings

1/3 cup Onion – chopped

1-4 Garlic cloves finely chopped

1 cup chopped carrots

1 cup chopped celery

1 Bay Leaf

½ teaspoon Fennel seeds, whole

1 ½ cup Green Lentils, washed and picked over (you can use French lentils but will need to adjust cooking time accordingly)

28 ounce can Whole Tomatoes with their liquid

22-32 ounces Water or Vegetable Broth (depending upon your taste for brothy vs. stew   type lentil soup.)

(Optional) 2 inch piece rind of Italian Grating cheese

(Optional) Crushed Hot Red Pepper to taste

(Optional) a few sprigs of celery greens finely chopped

Clean and chop all of the vegetables. Clean the lentils fist placing them in a colander under running water. Pick them over to remove impurities, place aside. Open the can of tomatoes, reserve liquid. Roughly chop tomatoes (or squeeze and break apart with hand) and place them aside.

Add the onion and sauté for 2 or 3 minutes, then add the garlic and (optional) crushed red pepper, sauté another minute.

Once the onions turn translucent add carrot, celery and bay leaf and fennel. Cover and lower flame to medium low, allow to sauté on low for 5 minutes.

Add the tomatoes (reserve the liquid), followed by the lentils to the pan. Allow to simmer for a minute or so, long enough for the flavors to combine. Add 1 cup of liquid (vegetable broth or water) and simmer for a minute.

Add remainder of liquid (and optional loosely chopped celery leaves). Bring to a rolling simmer, add (optional) grated cheese rind and lower the heat to low. Cover with lid slightly ajar on one edge. Stir every 20 minutes. Cook for one to one and a half hours.

To Serve: Cook some small pasta (like ditalini or shells), serve by placing just a little pasta in the center of a soup bowl. Place lentils over pasta and stir together. The lentils are the center point of the meal, the pasta is justa little added carbohydrate. Serve with fresh grated cheese and fresh cracked black pepper.

Rind of a Firm Italian grating Cheese: Types of commonly used Firm

Italian Grating Cheeses and the type of milk they are made from: Asiago (cow's milk), Parmigiano Reggiano (cow's milk), Pecorino Romano (my personal favorite grating cheese and favorite brand Locatelli, made from sheep's milk), Grana Padano (cow's milk). Add the rind to soup when it first comes to a rolling simmer, then continue to cook the recipe as you would. The addition of the rind accounts for a pervasive southern Italian cultural belief in wasting nothing and using and re-using everything. The addition of the rind also imparts a delightful, almost secretive, bottom flavor.

Chicken Soup naturally gluten free

Growing up in my house meant chicken soup was the prescription for every conceivable ailment related to cold weather. To me it seems logical that chicken soup will contain the vegetables which are abundant and readily available in any given location. The secret flavor my family uses is the addition of chopped celery greens. My grandmother and my great aunts often prepared a chicken stock prior to making soup. This is great to do on a really cold day; the smell of it cooking becomes very warm and homey. However, in the modern American lifestyle, we have limited time. We also have access to satisfying boxes of broths, stocks and soups. I usually only prepare homemade stock on a cold winter's weekend or for a special meal.

Quick Chicken Soup gluten free

Making a soup from scratch stock out of the question? Whole chicken too much - this is the soup for you! It is also great on work nights! Pictured with small rice flour dumplings, Mombriglio, recipe page 105.

Yields 4-6 servings

½ pound Chicken Cutlets or chicken pieces

¼- ½ bunch Italian Flat Leaf Parsley

1 stalk Celery, chopped

2 Carrots, chopped or cut into small rounds

3/4 cup Onion, chopped

Quick Chicken Soup *gluten free*

2 cloves Garlic, chopped

1 bunch Celery Leaves from stalks

1 Bay Leaf

32 ounces Chicken Stock or Broth (stock tastes better)

4 cups Water

Fresh Milled Black Pepper
Grated hard Italian Cheese to taste

Clean chicken. Set aside. Prepare vegetables. Chop celery, garlic, carrot and celery, leave aside separately. Chop parsley, leave aside. Chop celery leaves, place aside. Place cooking pot on stove top. Warm 1 tablespoon of olive oil in pot, add onions, sauté for 2 minutes. Add garlic, mix in and sauté for a moment. Add the optional hot pepper. Add chopped celery and onion. Add bay leaf. Sprinkle a pinch of salt on top of vegetables, stir and keep heat on medium low. Partially cover pot. Vegetables should sauté for about 4 minutes.

Move vegetables to sides of pan. Place chicken cutlets (or pieces) in center of pan. Raise heat to medium. Cook with partial cover for 3 minutes, flip chicken, and cook for another 3 minutes.

Pour 32 ounces of store bought stock or broth into pot. Stir and cook for a moment. Pour in 4 cups of water. Stir. Bring to a boil then reduce to a simmer. Add optional cheese rind and partially cover the pot. Allow to simmer for 45 minutes. Serve alone or with small pasta, fresh cracked pepper and grated cheese.

Sauces

I offer examples of sauces which are bold and thick, flavorful and gluten free. Either can be served over vegetables and more.

Béchamel gluten free

This is such a delicious creamy and smooth sauce. It is wonderful on vegetables, in gratins and on pasta dishes like lasagna. The pot and heat need to be watched closely until all of the ingredients become smooth, which creates the perfect consistency. The most important thing to do is keep the heat low and just keep whisking. There is a movement to create gluten free recipes which look like and resemble white bleached wheat flour. I am more concerned about flavor, it is important to remember that different flours cast different hues. I use a tablespoon of Sorghum flour in this recipe because it contributes significant wheat - type flavor. Sorghum, of any gluten free flour I am acquainted, tastes

Béchamel gluten free

most closely to wheat flour but it is very dry. Be cautious to not use too much. If you only have Potato Starch then substitute it for the Sorghum.

Yields 1 ½ cups

2 cups Milk

4 tablespoons Butter

1 tablespoon gluten free Sorghum Flour

2 tablespoons gluten free Potato Starch

1/8 teaspoon Salt

Pour 2 cups of milk in a container with a spout and leave aside for a while so it warms up to room temperature. Whisk together Sorghum and Potato Starch in a small bowl, completely combine and place aside.

Melt butter in a pot large enough to accommodate 2 cups of liquid. Be sure to keep heat on low. Melt the butter, do not allow butter to get too warm or turn color from heat which is too high. If butter browns the flours can burn and taste horrid. Allow the butter to melt thoroughly.

Gradually whisk in the flour mixture to the butter. I add 1 teaspoon of flour at a time. Whisk to thoroughly combine, then add another teaspoon. Do this until all of the flour has been added. The mixture in the pan should be thick and need to be moved constantly, or it can burn.

Very slowly begin whisking in the milk, pour it in a slow stream only a few tablespoons at a time. Continue to whisk, allowing the sauce to thicken between additions of milk. The heat is really important to watch. I sometimes turn the heat off for a moment or move the pot to a cold burner and continue whisking briskly. This also keeps clumps from forming. The texture you are looking to maintain is that of complete smoothness. As the mixture thickens to sauce, whisk in the salt. You will know when the sauce is done; it will be smooth, thick, rich and inviting.

Sunday Tomato Sauce gluten free

Salsa di Pomodoro Domenica senza glutine

A quick and traditional Sunday Sauce, simplicity at its best. The standard for any Neapolitan sauce is garlic, extra virgin olive oil, basil and tomatoes. It does not need to cook forever, just simmer long enough for the flavors to combine. A lot of families use onions or sugar to sweeten the acid of the tomatoes. I sometimes add a pinch of baking soda if the tomatoes are particularly acidic, a trick handed down from my paternal great grandmother.

Yields enough for 4-6 servings

3 cloves Garlic, finely chopped

2 teaspoons olive oil

28 ounce can Crushed Tomatoes

¼ teaspoon dried Basil

Pinch Salt

(Optional) Crushed Red Pepper to taste

(Optional) Grated Cheese to taste

(Optional) Fresh Milled Black Pepper to taste

Heat a heavy bottomed sauce pot to medium, add olive oil and allow it to warm. Add garlic and optional crushed red pepper, lower heat a bit. Allow garlic to wilt and just begin to turn color, add basil and allow herb to infuse the oil.

 Add the can of tomatoes, bring to a rolling simmer. Lower heat, cover with lid partially ajar. Stir every so often and allow sauce to simmer on low for 40 minutes. Add a pinch of salt before serving.

 If the tomatoes have a lot of liquid add a tablespoon or more of tomato paste, but this is rarely necessary when using "crushed" tomatoes. Serve with optional grated cheese and fresh milled pepper.

Pasta

"A Watched Pot Never Boils..."

My dear Great Aunt, Zia Vincenza Ruggiero Anzelone would say "a watched pot never boils." She would watch me watch the pot of water, waiting for it to boil. She would also watch as I would anxiously stir the pasta and incessantly test it for readiness; she would laugh and ask me what I was waiting for. I'd usually whine something about being hungry. She'd laugh again and say "you know- a watched pot never boils". I would reply, "Uuughhh!" She wouldn't make me move nor get angry – she would just laugh. "What does that even mean?!" I would bellow back. She would say, "you think about it, and you will understand." How many times in my life I have had a moment to reflect upon this truth. Once I have prepared anything in life, I must let it loose into the world and wait for it to fruit. I must wait for the attention and energy I placed into it to take effect. I've learned to live in awareness of the moment and wait for the magic to happen, because a watched pot never boils.

When I first began Gluten Free living and cooking, there were not many tasteful brands of gluten free pasta available. In fact many of the brands, once minimally cooked, are a mushy gross mess. I require pasta that tastes authentic. It must have the texture of traditional Italian pastas I was raised with. There are a number of pastas from Italy, often corn based, but processed in a way which closely mimic Italian durum semolina (wheat) pasta. In my opinion, the flavor always depends on the brand and the manufacturing process, not necessarily the ingredients. Gluten free pasta needs to be closely watched as it goes from "al dente" to mush within the blink of an eye. I do not always follow the cook time on the label; I use the watchful eye instead. In general, once you see an enormous starch release, the pasta is almost ready.

Cooking time and a lot of water are dramatically important with gluten free pasta; time can vary greatly amongst brands and shapes. Ample water brought to a rolling simmer, indicates it is time to add Salt. Salt helps keep pasta from sticking to itself and adds flavor to the final dish. Salt does not speed cooking time. Add salt when the water begins to simmer, this is when the water is hot enough to burn off the oxygen in the water. Otherwise the chemical reaction of oxygen and salt (sodium chloride) can pit stainless steel pan surfaces. My grandmother used to say that the pasta water should be as salty as the Mediterranean Sea. Once salt is added, bring water to a rolling boil then gradually gluten free pasta, stir often and cook until al dente. At the time pasta has cooked, it will release a surge of starch. This is your "heads up", if the pasta continues to cook too far past this it can potentially become a mushy mess. This is a key variant from traditional wheat based pasta.

Pasta is done when it has a good tooth, *al dente*. Pasta with tooth has bite and some chew. It is NOT a coagulated mush. My dad and I liked pasta cooked the same way. Today, in the study of the glycemic index we learn that carbohydrates which have thick density take longer to digest, thereby keeping our blood sugar from spiking as quickly as when we eat mushy carbohydrate.

Pasta with Sausage & Ricotta gluten free

Serves 4

2 links hot or sweet Sausage with Fennel with minimal fat

3 Garlic cloves, finely chopped

2 cups Ricotta Cheese

1 tablespoon Extra Virgin Olive Oil

1 pound Cooked gluten free Pasta

¾ cup Pasta Cooking Water, reserved

3 tablespoons Grated Cheese

(Optional) Crushed Red Pepper to taste

Remove sausage casings. In a pot, cook the sausage crumbles. Add the finely chopped garlic and the optional crushed red pepper to the sausage, cook all thoroughly.

Boil water and cook the pasta while making ricotta sauce. When pasta is a couple of minutes from cooked, use a measuring cup and scoop out ¾ cup of pasta water, be sure the water is cloudy. The cloudiness is starch, which will help the cheese sauce thicken. Set aside. Drain the pasta when cooked, set aside for a moment.

When pasta is a couple of minutes from being done, turn pan with sausage back on. Use a measuring cup and scoop out ¾ cup of pasta water, be sure the water is cloudy. The cloudiness is starch, which will help the cheese sauce to thicken.

Using a spoon to mix and combine all of the ingredients in the pan gently. Once the mixture has turned into a sauce, add the t grated cheese and more of the optional crushed red pepper. Add the pasta to the pan with the sauce. Combine and stir. Transfer to pasta bowls. Serve with salad and a vegetable.

Pasta with Ricotta gluten free

Pasta with Ricotta is Italian macaroni and cheese at its best; either Gluten Free Pasta or gluten rich pasta can be used. This dish is often called "Shepherd's Pasta". I enjoy it cooked with crumbled previously cooked sausage, although without meat is delicious as well.

3 Garlic cloves, finely chopped

2 cups Ricotta Cheese

1 tablespoon Extra Virgin Olive Oil

1 pound cooked gluten free Pasta (penne, farfalle, fusilli)

½ cup Pasta Cooking Water, reserved

3 tablespoons Grated Cheese

(Optional) Crushed Red Pepper to taste

Using a heavy bottomed pot, add 1 tablespoon of olive oil to the pan. Add the finely chopped garlic and the optional crushed red pepper to the pan and sauté.

Boil water and cook the pasta while making ricotta sauce. When pasta is a couple of minutes from cooked, use a measuring cup and scoop out ¾ cup of pasta water, be sure the water is cloudy. The cloudiness is starch, which will help the cheese sauce thicken. Set aside. Drain the pasta when cooked, set aside for a moment.

Add a little water from the reserved pasta water to the sauté and let the water sizzle. Immediately follow with the ricotta, followed by the rest of the pasta water. Pour the water directly into the ricotta.

Using a wooden spoon, mix and combine all of the ingredients in the pan gently. Once the mixture has turned into a sauce, add the grated cheese and more of the optional crushed red pepper.

Add the pasta to the pan with the sauce. Combine and stir.

Transfer to pasta bowls. Serve with salad and a vegetable.

Pasta Puttanesca gluten free

This Puttanesca (or whore's sauce in Neapolitan) is fast, hot and quick! Just perfect for a quick work night meal! I often add more parsley than noted in this recipe. Also, for a protein packed meal, toss a can of drained Italian tuna in olive oil with the pasta, followed by the sauce.

Yields 3-4 servings

28 ounce can of Crushed Tomatoes

4 finely chopped crushed Garlic cloves

2 tablespoons gluten free Capers (drained)

½ cup (about 16) Kalamata olives (pitted and halved or quartered lengthwise)

1 tin (about 11) Anchovies, finely chopped

½ cup of Parsley

2 teaspoons Extra Virgin Olive Oil

Crushed Red Pepper to taste

Salt to taste

Freshly milled Black Pepper

12 ounces gluten free Pasta

Bring water for pasta to boil. Sauté garlic & crushed red pepper in olive oil in a sauté pan. I like it hot – do you like it hot? Add the crushed red pepper to the oil at the start infuses the oil with the chili and the heat.

   Once the garlic wilts and the oil is distinctly tinged red (or not if you don't like too much heat), then add the can of crushed tomatoes. Once it comes to a rolling simmer reduce heat. Allow the sauce to simmer 10-15 minutes. Add 1/3 cup parsley, capers & olives. Cook another couple of minutes.

   Serve with the remaining fresh parsley atop the fresh servings, with freshly milled black pepper.

Pasta with Walnut Paste gluten free

This is a great comfort food. So quick and easy, great for work nights – prepare the paste while the pasta cooks! Years ago this would be made with a mortar and pestle, I use my food processor for a quick spin to pound and combine the ingredients. I observed after taking the photos of this dish, that it looks like a summer pasta. I assure you, the addition of butter to the walnut paste makes it a cold weather sort of meal.

12 ounces gluten free Pasta

½ cup + 2 tablespoons Walnuts

2 tablespoons gluten free plain Breadcrumbs

Pasta with Walnut Paste gluten free

3 teaspoons Extra Virgin Olive Oil

3 tablespoons Italian Flat Leaf Parsley

1 Garlic clove

2 tablespoons Butter, softened

1 tablespoon Cream or Milk

Salt & fresh milled Pepper to taste

3 teaspoons Italian Hard Grating Cheese

Boil water for pasta. While the water comes to a boil, make the walnut paste. Use a food processor or blender, process the ingredients into a paste, in this order: Garlic, parsley, nuts,

1 teaspoon grated cheese, Extra Virgin Olive Oil. (You can use a mortar and pestle in the old method, in which case you will need to chop the walnuts to a fine meal first and add them to the paste in the same order of ingredients.) Be sure to scrape down the sides of the food processor bowl between additions of ingredients.

Add the pasta to the boiling water and cook.

Place the butter in a bowl large enough to accommodate the pasta. Use the back of a spoon to mix the butter and walnut paste. Add the walnut paste to the butter, combine thoroughly and add cream or milk to loosen.

Drain the pasta and add it to the walnut butter paste, the heat of the pasta will warm the paste and melt the butter thoroughly. Add the grated cheese to the pasta, toss pasta again. Then add salt and pepper to taste.

I serve this with a salad. I include some chopped walnut on the salad for this meal. Enjoy!

Mombriglio Gluten Free

Small Dumplings for Brothy Soups

No one knows where my grandmother (Yolanda Ruggiero) came up with or acquired this recipe - Mombriglio is sort of its own family legend. Mombriglio are small dumpling like pasta. They are hardy and especially delicious on cold winter days. They are delicious in any brothy soup. I grew up with them in chicken soup (chicken soup recipe page 101). These store well, I place them in an air tight container and leave in the refrigerator for up to four days. Stored in an airtight container these little dumplings freeze for a month.

This recipe was originally designed to use cream of wheat and as a result I had given up these little dumplings. One recent winter day my mom called and invited me for an dinner, she said she had a special surprise for me. She made chicken soup with Mombriglio, using cream of rice instead of the wheat. It so warmed my heart! This gluten free culinary cultural evolution comes from my mom, Marianna Ruggiero Gamache.

Yields enough dumplings for 4 quarts of soup

1 cup gluten free Cream of Rice

2 whole Eggs

1 Egg Yolk

½ cup Flat Leaf Italian Parsley finely chopped

1/3 cup Italian Grated Cheese

Preheat the oven to 300 degrees. Retrieve a cookie sheet or jelly roll pan and place aside.

Place cream of rice in a large mixing bowl. Add the grated cheese and stir with tines of a dinner fork. Add 2 eggs, plus 1 yolk, one at a time. Mix with fork. Add finely chopped parsley, stir with fork.

Using your hands, crumble pea and quarter sized crumbles directly onto cookie sheet or jelly roll pan. Sometimes you have to squeeze some of it to clump together. Place leftover crumbles on pan as well. Space all apart so they can dry well.

Place cookie sheet in oven. Bake 35 minutes. The goal is to dry them out so they hold their own. Their surface will feel *almost* crisp, definitely solid and they will hold their shape with ease. Remove from oven and cool.

To Use Mombriglio in a Brothy Soup

When Mombriglio are added directly to the cooking pot, they bulk up the soup up to a stew. My mom prefers it this way. I prefer a brothy soup, so I ladle out the amount of soup for the meal into a separate pot and cook the Mombriglio from there. Either way the cooking method is the same: Return soup to a rolling simmer. Add 1 handful per bowl of soup to be dished out. Reduce to a slight simmer, allow to cook for 17 minutes. Turn off heat and allow to sit a few minutes. Ladle into soup bowl and enjoy!

Storage: When there is no warmth they are ready to use or store. They keep best in an airtight container. Keep unused in the fridge for a few days or in the freezer up to a month.

Mombriglio full gluten

This is the recipe that has been part of my life since childhood. They turn soup into a hearty meal on cold wintery days! I grew up with this cream of wheat version.

Yields enough dumplings for 4 quarts of soup

1 cup Cream of Wheat

2 whole Eggs

½ cup Flat Leaf Italian Parsley finely chopped

1/4 cup Grated Cheese

Splash of Water

Preheat the oven to 300 degrees. Place a jelly roll pan (the sides can be helpful but are not necessary), or a cookie sheet to the side.

Place cream of wheat in a large mixing bowl.   Add the grated cheese and stir with tines of a dinner fork.   Add 2 eggs, one at a time. Mix with fork.   Add finely chopped parsley, stir with fork. If mixture is too dry, drizzle in a splash of water.

Using your hands, crumble pea and quarter sized crumbles directly onto cookie sheet or jelly roll pan. Place leftover crumbles on pan as well. Space the dumplings apart to dry well. Place cookie sheet in oven. Bake 25 minutes. The goal is to dry them out so they hold their own. Their surface will feel almost crisp, definitely solid, and they should hold their shape with ease.

Remove from oven and cool. When there is no warmth they are ready to use, or to be stored in an airtight container.

Baked Pasta Recipes

Pastieri gluten free

Baked Pasta with Egg & Grated Cheese

This baked pasta dish is the same recipe for gluten free pasta and traditional pasta. The pasta must have tooth (be "al dente") at the end of the boiling process. Pasta with "tooth", has enough chewiness to allow the pasta to move in the liquid fluidly but it should still have a thick center of uncooked dough. The pasta will continue to cook while it bakes in the oven. If you boil the pasta and cook it in full before baking, the final product will be a mushy mess.

When I was lacto-ovo vegetarian, my former mother in law Raffaela Vacchio, would often make this dish for me. It comes from her home in Avellino Italy. She would add a lot of hot crushed red pepper at my urging while preparing the egg

Pastieri gluten free

mixture. *I found myself as an adult in her kitchen, often feeling like a girl with my elders learning the ways of old. She once told me that the dish used to be served when meat was scarce. She went on to say that we are lucky in America to have markets that always have a constant supply of meat available to shoppers.*

This is a country dish and useful at time when "the hens are laying" and eggs are bountiful. Many countryside Italian dishes exist for this reason coupled with the need to provide adequate protein for one's entire family when meat, or money for meat, is not bountiful.

I like this as a mid-day or early evening meal, as it is heavy and needs to be burned off. It is delicious with a salad. (It also keeps well for camping - I place a piece on the grill to warm it up.) This dish is great because it is delicious warm from the oven as well as at room temperature.

Yields one 9 x 10" baking dish

1 pound gluten free pasta (something long and flat)

3 tablespoons Extra-Virgin Olive Oil

Egg Mixture:

7 Eggs

¼ teaspoon Granulated Garlic

1/8 teaspoon Salt

¼ cup Grated Cheese

(Optional) Crushed Red Pepper

Use a baking dish large enough to accommodate one pound of pasta. This is usually done in a tray shape or a shallow large bowl. Pour a few drops of olive oil in the bowl and use paper to spread across entire surface, pre-heat oven to 350 degrees.

Boil water for pasta. Place enough water in a large pan to cook pasta. Salt water when water begins to simmer, add oil, add uncooked pasta.

Prepare the egg mixture in a separate bowl. Whisk together eggs, add garlic, salt, (the optional crushed red pepper), 1 tablespoon of olive oil, and ¼ cup finely grated cheese. Whisk all ingredients together.

Add the uncooked pasta to the boiling water. Cook pasta for about ¾ of the total cooking time. Ultimately, you are looking for a heavy "tooth". Please read above information for full detail of the tooth.

Using a heat resistant measuring cup, just before pasta is drained, retain about 1 cup of cooking water and place aside. Drain pasta and then place it back in pan it was cooked in..

Add 1 tablespoon of olive oil to the pasta and toss. Sprinkle pasta with some grated cheese and toss. Slowly temper the reserved cooking water to the egg mixture. Then add whisked water and egg mixture to the pasta. Toss the pasta to completely coat. The mixture should just cover the pasta.

Add pasta to the oiled baking bowl or tray. Place in center of pre-heated oven. Cover and bake covered for 20 minutes. Then uncover and bake for 20-25 minutes. It is cooked when small bubbles at the sides of the food can be seen and the center is spongy to the touch. Allow to set and cool for at least 25 minutes before eating. Enjoy hot or at room temperature. I enjoy this as a meal with a salad.

Lasagne gluten free

Baked Pasta with 3 Cheeses in Tomato Sauce

I grew up eating gluten rich flour and used to make Lasagne by boiling the noodles first. In later years, I moved to the no boil method. My experience has demonstrated that Gluten Free Lasagna pasta does not lend well to pre-cooking. Just use gluten free lasagna noodles as no boil. The no boil noodle approach requires considerably more moisture for gluten free than it does for wheat pasta. The bottom layer has the most moisture added, as it will set a steam reaction in place during baking. I use the Sunday Tomato Sauce recipe on page 105. Enjoy this delicious Lasagna recipe.

Ricotta Mixture:

2 pounds whole milk Ricotta

2 whole Eggs

3 tablespoons Grated Cheese

¼ pound shredded Mozzarella

For the Layers:

Approximately 13 ounces gluten free Lasagna Noodles

¾ pound shredded Mozzerella

3-4 tablespoons Grated Cheese

4 ½ cups previously prepared Tomato Sauce, a thinner sauce

3 tablespoons (scant) of water

Preheat the oven to 350 degrees. Use a deep baking dish or roasting pan approximately 7" x 13". Prepare *Ricotta Mixture* by placing all ingredients in a mixing bowl and combine well. Place aside.

Ladle 1 ½ cups of sauce into the bottom of the baking dish, add to it scant 3 tablespoons of water. Use a spoon to quickly mix and combine. The extra water is for steam action that will build up during baking, it is not nearly enough to interfere with flavor. Place a layer of noodles across bottom. Allow the curly ends of the pasta to overlap.

Place dollops of ricotta mixture across previously placed lasagna noodles. Smooth with back of spoon to completely cover entire surface. It is very important to layer the cheese to the sides of the pan; this creates a moisture barrier which supports the gluten free pasta in cooking evenly and to having rubbery texture when done.

Place another layer of lasagna over ricotta mixture. Break pasta with hand to make the correct size. Stuff the broken pieces of pasta at ends, sides and corners, covering the entire surface. Place the second layer in a different direction than the first. I find this makes the pasta hold even better shape for serving.

Ladle another 1 ½ cups of tomato sauce to cover uncooked pasta. Sprinkle some grated cheese and dollop another round of ricotta over the sauce layer, being sure again to get the cheese to the ends of the pan.

Finally, place one last layer of dry lasagna pasta over the ricotta mixture, in the same direction as the first layer of pasta, being sure to place pasta to the side of dish. Ladle another 1 ½ cups of tomato sauce over the pasta. Sprinkle with some grated cheese and crumble shredded mozzarella across top.

Cover with foil, crimped at ends. Bake covered for 35 minutes in the center of the oven.   Check lasagna for dryness, ladle a few tablespoons of sauce around edges that seem dry. Place foil back on, crimp sides. Bake for another 15 minutes.

Uncover and bake for an additional 7 minutes. Remove from oven, allow to rest at least 30 minutes before attempting to cut into it.

Lasagne full gluten

When I still ate gluten rich flour, I used to make Lasagne by boiling the noodles first; you can use no bake. Wheat lasagna pasta does not need the same amount of moisture as gluten free pasta requires. Therefore the recipes are separate.

Ricotta Mixture:

2 pounds whole milk Ricotta

2 whole Eggs

3 tablespoons Grated Cheese

¼ pound shredded Mozzarella

For the Layers:

1 pound No Bake Lasagna Noodles

¾ pound shredded Mozzarella

3-4 tablespoons Grated Cheese

2 ½ cups previously prepared Tomato Sauce

Preheat the oven to 350 degrees. Use a deep baking dish or roasting pan. Prepare Ricotta Mixture, by placing all ingredients in a mixing bowl and combine well. Place aside.

Ladle a layer of Tomato Sauce over bottom of pan. Sprinkle a bit of grated cheese over sauce. Then place enough noodles to cover sauce, allow lasagna to overlap about ¼ of an inch. Place dollops of ricotta mixture across previously placed lasagna noodles. Smooth with back of spoon to completely cover entire surface.

Add another lasagna layer, ladle ½ cup of tomato sauce to cover lasagna. Sprinkle some grated cheese. Then add a layer of shredded mozzarella. Repeat and assemble another layer. The final top layer will require ¾ cup of tomato sauce and a final layer of shredded mozzarella.

Cover with foil and bake covered for 25 minutes. Uncover and bake another 20 minutes until rolling bubbles of sauce and steam are visible along sides. Allow to rest and set for at least 20 minutes before serving.

Baked Ziti gluten free

This is an oldie but goodie. Baked pasta recipes require the pasta boiling time be cut short by several minutes; this is the same for gluten rich or gluten free pasta. Baked Ziti is quite hardy and not an everyday dish. It can be made with part skim milk cheeses, but truthfully it takes away flavor. I use the Sunday Tomato Sauce recipe on page 105.

12-16 ounces gluten free Ziti (or Penne or other short round pasta)

1 ½ pounds Ricotta

16 ounces Mozzarella, shredded

2 tablespoons Grated hard Italian Cheese

2 whole Eggs, beaten

2-3 cups of prepared Tomato Sauce

Pre-heat oven to 350 degrees, place a 3quart oven safe baking dish to the side. Beat two eggs, place aside. In a large Pasta pot, boil water for pasta and cook pasta for three quarters of the required cooking time, then strain.

While the pasta cooks, prepare the ricotta mixture. Add the ricotta to an empty mixing bowl. Use a spoon to mix the ricotta which softens and makes it smooth. Mix in the grated cheese, followed by the beaten eggs. Mix in 10-12 ounces of the shredded mozzarella fold over until well dispersed. Place aside.

Add the partially cooked pasta to the ricotta mixture and stir until all pasta is completely coated. Place entire mixture into the baking dish. Crumble remaining shredded mozzarella over surface of pasta.

Cover and place in center of pre-heated oven. Bake for 25 minutes covered, then uncover and bake an additional 10 minutes, until bubbling at edges. Let the ziti rest for at least 20 minutes to set before serving. Left overs taste even better!

Cookies

Biscotti

I am not the only food enthusiast in my family, I am grateful to come from a long line of amazing foodies and keepers of ancestral kitchen wisdom. My beautiful and amazing cousin, Linda Cuono, has been an enormous influence for me in the kitchen and in life. Linda's kindness and willingness to discuss food and matters of the heart make her extraordinary. She has always taken time to bestow her Kitchen Wisdom. Without her wisdom and the wisdom of our Ancestors, biscotti would not be in my life or in this book.

I pride myself in baking a product which is moist and well structured, not crumbly. I do not believe that gluten free baking should be dry, unless the traditional recipe is designed to be so. Southern Italians love dry cookies (biscotti) as well as moist. Therefore, some traditional recipes are dryer because that is what the culinary culture created many generations ago. Some flavors particular to the Southern Italian palate are: anise, citrus and nut. Citrus flavors are common and lemons, citron, orange or orange flower water often appear. Nut flavors touch the palate in overtones or undertones and are very common using almond, hazelnut, pignoli (pine nuts) or walnut.

I have chosen to include the traditional gluten rich recipes with a twofold purpose. As a learning tool, I find the original recipe very helpful. I believe the inclusion of the original gluten rich recipes is important for those of us who originally learned to bake using gluten rich flour. Additionally, the inclusion of the original gluten rich recipes is my action in preserving the culinary culture I was raised with. I believe their inclusion contributes to the international movement of cultural preservation, particular to the Province of Caserta in the Campania Region of Italy. For more information, please visit Chapter One "Culinary Cultural Evolution."

Zia Maria's Sesame Cookies gluten free

Biscotti Sesame di Zia Maria

This particular cookie is so entrenched in our culture that one cannot visit a Southern Italian American bakery without seeing these delicious treats behind the counter. I grew up with these cookies. Seemingly every kitchen on my mom's side makes these scrumptious Sesame Cookies! This recipe came to me from my Great Aunt Maria Ruggiero Cuono. The Gluten Free and full gluten versions of this recipe each call for a lot of cold butter. Cutting the cold butter into the flour with a pastry blender forms air pockets; this allows the cookie to be light. The sorghum, eggs and sesame seed pack a lot of protein into this yummy cookie. This sesame cookie recipe adds the wet ingredients in an odd placement, the addition of moisture at the end allows for crystallization which will contribute to the crispness of the cookies. This cookie is meant to be crisp, the older it gets the better it tastes ... at least that's what my elders used to say.

Yields approximately 30 cookies

2/3 cup gluten free Sorghum Flour

¾ cup gluten free Potato Starch

2/3 cup gluten free Brown Rice Flour

2 teaspoon gluten free Baking Powder

1 teaspoon gluten free Guar Gum

¼ teaspoon Salt

¾ cup Sugar

12 tablespoons Cold Butter – cubed

2 tablespoons gluten free Tahini (Sesame butter)

2 Egg Yolks

¼ cup Milk

2 teaspoons gluten free Vanilla extract

1/3 cup Sesame Seeds

Preheat oven to 375 degrees.

Sift sorghum flour, brown rice flour, potato starch, baking powder, guar gum and salt into a large mixing bowl. Cut the cold butter into cubes. Place the milk, egg yolks and vanilla in a bowl or cup with a spout. Use fork to beat and mix the liquids together. Leave aside

Add 1/3 of the cubed butter into the bowl. Using a pastry blender, cut cubed butter into flour until the texture turns into coarse crumbs. Push the pastry blender into the butter, run a butter knife parallel to the wires of the blender to cut butter back into the flour. Continue to add butter and blend in two more batches.

Cut in the tahini, thoroughly blend to coarse crumbs. Add the sugar. Do so ¼ cup at a time, blending after each addition of sugar. Use the pastry blender to scoop down the sides of the bowl.

Slowly add the egg and milk mixture until the dough holds together. Using the pastry blender work the moisture into all of the dough. If dough is too wet, add a tablespoon of potato starch.

Place the sesame seeds in a very shallow bowl or plate. Using a tablespoon, scoop a scant tablespoon of dough out of bowl. Shape between palms of hands into an oblong shape. Roll on three sides in the sesame seed. Make cookies about 1 – 1 ½ inches in length, longer will require additional cooking time.

Place directly on clean cookie sheet. I place the cookies on a diagonal with about 2 inches in between each cookie.

Bake for 15 minutes, or until golden light brown. Remove from oven.

Leave on cookie sheet and allow cooling and setting for a minute or so before removing to wire racks.

Once cookies are completely cool, store in a cookie lined wax paper. Cover with wax paper, after a few days the tin lid can be used. If you seal lid completely the moisture will make the cookie soft.

Zia Maria's Sesame Cookies full gluten

Yields approximately 30 cookies

2 cups Sifted All Purpose Flour

1 ½ teaspoon Baking Powder

¼ teaspoon Salt

¾ cup Sugar

2/3 cup Cold Butter – cubed

2 Egg Yolks

¼ cup Milk

1 ½ teaspoon Vanilla

1/3 cup Sesame Seeds

Preheat oven to 375 degrees.

Sift flour, baking powder and salt into a large mixing bowl.

Cut the cold butter into cubes. Place the milk, egg yolks and vanilla in a bowl or cup with a spout. Use fork to beat and mix the liquids together. Leave aside

Place 1/3 of the butter into the bowl. Using a pastry blender, cut cubed butter into flour until the texture turns into coarse crumbs. Push the pastry blender into the butter, run a butter knife parallel to the wires of the blender to cut butter back into the flour. Continue to add butter and blend in two more batches.

Once the texture turns to coarse crumbs, add the sugar. Do so ¼ cup at a time, blending after each addition of sugar. Use the pastry blender to scoop down the sides of the bowl.

Slowly add the egg and milk mixture until the dough holds together. Using the pastry blender work the moisture into all of the dough.

Place the sesame seeds in a very shallow bowl or plate.

Using a tablespoon, scoop a scant tablespoon of dough out of bowl. Shape between palms of hands into an oblong log shape. Roll on three sides in the sesame seed.

Place directly on clean cookie sheet. I place the cookies on a diagonal with about 2 inches in between each cookie.

Bake for 17 minutes, or until golden light brown. Remove from oven.

Leave on cookie sheet and allow to cool for 5 minutes.

Remove cookies to wire racks to cool. The recipe yields approximately 2 ½ dozen biscotti.

Once completely cool, store in a cookie lined with wax paper. Cover with wax paper, after a few days the tin lid can be used. If you seal lid completely the moisture will make the cookie soft.

Pastry Blender: A *pastry blender* is a kitchen tool which is used to mix cold and hard butter or fat into flour to make pastry. The tool has a center handle and moon shaped wire strips that attach at each end of the handle. In this recipe the act of cutting the butter into the flour is what provides for a light baked product.   A pastry blender allows one to cut into flour evenly sized pieces of butter. The flour coats the butter. Cutting butter into flour keeps the butter intact before baking. In this recipe, the butter coated in flour will create steam pockets which contribute to the light texture. The critical chemistry while making the dough is to not allow the butter to melt. A stand mixer tends to melt the butter. A food processor might not melt the butter as much, but I have not found an alternative to the old fashioned act of cutting butter into the flour.

Pizzelle gluten free

Seemingly everyone on my mom's side of the family makes Pizzelle. One needs a Pizzelle maker to accomplish this product. Like a waffle iron, it is fitted with plates which are the historic lace shape. Thin and crisp, these can be made as a flat cookie or one can shape it as a cone for ice cream.

This is a great example of how to create light crispness in delicate baking with gluten free ingredients. Learning how to manipulate batter to be crisp or light is something we take for granted with full gluten baking. In this recipe, I chose to use egg yolk and a bit of sugar whipped fast for a moment to start the batter. This combination of yolk and sugar contributes to Pizzelle's crispness, the melted butter at the end keeps the batter from getting too heavy quickly and the combination produces a light product at the end. I use starch in this recipe as a binder. Sorghum contributes protein and a reminiscent flavor of wheat. I hope you enjoy these light and sweet treats!

Vanilla Pizzelle gluten free

Yields Approximately 2 Dozen

3 whole Eggs, separated

¾ cup Sugar

3 teaspoon gluten free Vanilla Extract

1/3 cup gluten free Sorghum Flour

2/3 cup gluten free White Rice Flour

1/2 cup gluten freePotato Starch

1 teaspoon gluten free Baking Powder

½ teaspoon gluten free Guar Gum

1/8 teaspoon Salt

¾ cup Butter, melted

Follow instructions for your Pizzelle maker, see information box on this page.

Separate the eggs. Melt the butter.

Whisk the dry ingredients (flours, starch, baking powder, guar gum and salt) in a separate bowl until thoroughly combined. Set aside.

Place all the yolk in the bowl of mixer, begin beating, add 2 tablespoons of the sugar. Whip for about 15 seconds. Lower mixer to medium, slowly add egg whites, and beat on medium high for about 15 seconds.

Keep mixer on medium. Slowly and gradually add the remaining sugar until well combined. Slowly and gradually, add the dry ingredients. Scrape down the batter from the side of mixing bowl periodically until just well combined.

Gradually mix the melted butter into the batter at the end, be sure to completely combine. The batter should be batter like and not too thick. If too

Vanilla Pizzelle gluten free

thick, add a splash of milk (dairy, soy or nut milk – a milk with protein and fat).

Plug in Pizzelle maker and warm to manufacturer instructions. Add the vanilla extract last and mix until just combined. Do not over aerate batter.

Once warm enough, butter the Pizzelle grills. I keep a stick of cold butter handy and just swipe it along the surface as needed. Spoon a bit more than a tablespoon of batter onto the center of each circle on the grill. My grill has two 6" circles. If your maker has smaller circles you will need to play around with the correct measurement of batter. You may also have to experiment with the exact location within the circle to place the batter. The goal is to get a perfect circle which does not pour out onto the side of the maker. The trick is really to know your maker.

Once the batter stops steaming, they are done. This only takes about 30 seconds. Catch them as they are crisp and light, or golden. Not brown.

Use a fork to pick up on end and gently lift and begin peeling back. I use my hand as well, peel back and transfer to wire cooling rack. They do not take long to completely cool. Once cooled, they can be stacked.

They tend to not be completely even at the circumference outer edge of cookie. To resolve this, wait until they are completely cooled. Hold Pizzelle in one hand; use the other hand to hold the side of the fork to the uneven edge. Very gently scrape the uneven crumbs off the entire circumference to get a smooth and even edge. I scrape the crumbles into a bowl and use the scrapings as an ice cream topping.

Storage: parchment or wax paper lined bakery box. Stack opposite side to opposite side. They keep like this for a week. *To serve*: sprinkle with powdered sugar.

Anise Pizzelle gluten free

Yields Approximately 2 Dozen

3 whole Eggs, separated

¾ cup Sugar

3 teaspoons gluten free Anise Extract

1/3 cup gluten free Sorghum Flour

2/3 cup gluten free White Rice Flour

1/2 cup gluten free Potato Starch

1 teaspoon gluten free Baking Powder

½ teaspoon gluten free Guar Gum

1/8 teaspoon Salt

¾ cup Butter, melted

Follow instructions for your Pizzelle maker, see information box on this page.
    Separate the eggs. Melt the butter.

Combine all of the dry ingredients (sorghum, white rice flour, potato starch, baking powder, guar gum and salt) in a separate bowl. Mix thoroughly. Set aside.

Place all the yolk in the bowl of mixer, begin beating, add 2 tablespoons of the sugar. Whip for about 15 seconds.

Lower mixer to medium, slowly add egg whites, beat on medium high for about 15 seconds. Keep mixer on medium. Slowly and gradually add the remaining sugar until well combined.

Slowly and gradually, add the dry ingredients. Scrape down the batter from the side of mixing bowl periodically until just well combined.

Gradually mix the melted butter into the batter at the end, be sure to completely combine. The batter should be batter like and not too thick. If too thick, add a splash of milk (dairy, soy or nut milk – a milk with protein and fat).

Plug in pizzelle maker and warm to manufacturer instructions. Mix in the anise extract last, do not over aerate batter.

 Once warm enough, butter the Pizzelle grills. I keep a stick of cold butter handy and just swipe it along the surface as needed.

Spoon a bit more than a tablespoon of batter onto the center of each circle on the grill. My grill has two 6" circles. If your maker has smaller circles you will need to play around with the correct measurement of batter. You may also have to experiment with the exact location within the circle to place the batter. The goal is to get a perfect circle which does not pour out onto the side of the maker. The trick is really to know your maker.

Once the batter stops steaming, they are done. This only takes about 30 seconds. Catch them as they are crisp and light, or golden. Not brown. Use a fork to pick up on end and gently lift and begin peeling back. I use my hand as well, peel back and transfer to wire cooling rack. They do not take long to completely cool. Once cooled, they can be stacked.

They tend to not be completely even at the circumference outer edge of cookie. To resolve this, wait until they are completely cooled. Hold Pizzelle in one hand, use the other hand to hold the side of the fork to the uneven edge. Very gently scrape the uneven crumbs off the entire circumference to get a smooth and even edge. I scrape the crumbles into a bowl and use the scrapings as an ice cream topping.

Storage: parchment or wax paper lined bakery box. Stack opposite side to opposite side. They keep like this for a week.   *To serve:* sprinkle with powdered sugar.

Anise Pizzelle full gluten

3 Eggs, beaten

¾ cup Sugar

¾ cup Butter, melted

1 ¾ cup All-Purpose Flour

1 teaspoon Baking Powder

2 teaspoons Vanilla Extract

1 teaspoon Anise Extract

Beat the eggs, mix in the sugar in a gentle stream.

Temper in the melted butter.

Add the flour and baking powder. Thoroughly combine, do not overmix.

Mix in the extracts. The batter should be batter like and not too thick. If too thick, add a splash of milk.

Follow instructions for your Pizzelle maker, once warm enough, butter the pizzelle grills. I keep a stick of cold butter handy and just swipe it along the surface as needed.

Spoon a bit more than a tablespoon of batter onto the center of each circle on the grill. My grill has two 6" circles. If your maker has smaller circles you will need to play around with the correct measurement of batter. You may also have to experiment with the exact location within the circle to place the batter. The goal is to get a perfect circle which does not pour out onto the side of the maker. The trick is really to know your maker.

Once the batter stops steaming, they are done. This only takes about 30 seconds. Catch them as they are crisp and light, or golden. Not brown.

Use a fork to pick up on end and gently lift and begin peeling back. I use my hand as well, peel back and transfer to wire cooling rack. They do not take long to completely cool. Once cooled, they can be stacked.

They tend to not be completely even at the circumference outer edge of cookie. To resolve this, wait until they are completely cooled. Hold pizzelle in one hand, use the other hand to hold the side of the fork (or a butter knife) up to the uneven edge. Very gently scrape the uneven crumbs off the entire circumference to get a smooth and even edge.

Storage: parchment or wax paper lined bakery box. Stack opposite side to opposite side. They keep like this for over a week. To serve: sprinkle with powdered sugar.

Pizzelle Variations:

These can be made in many flavors. The flavors I offer are my favorites, but you can replace the extract with any different flavor of your choice (lemon, almond, hazelnut, etc.)

Know Your Pizzelle Maker: Pay close attention to how your Pizzelle maker works. Plug it in and allow it to warm with a closed lid to preheat. Brush grids with butter before use, an even circle with little runoff is desired. Placement of batter is key and different with each maker. Some Pizzelle makers work well placing batter in the center of the circle, some makers work best if batter is off-center. Cook Pizzelle until steaming stops, this should only take a number of seconds (my maker requires 30 seconds). If Pizzelle are too brown they taste different. Light and just turning a golden hue is best.

Lady Kisses gluten free

Baci di Dama *senza glutine*

Lady Kisses are nut meal butter cookies common in Italian American Bakeries. This is a hearty cookie that can stand alone or with chocolate. They are very delicious, rich and high in protein. I use almond meal, however this cookie transcends many nut flavors and just about any nut meal can be used.

Yields Approximately 4 dozen individual cookies

Cookie Dough:

11 tablespoons Butter (room temperature)

¾ cup Sugar

1 Whole Egg (not cold)

1 teaspoon gluten free Almond Extract

1 cup Fine Ground Almond Meal*

½ cup + 2 tablespoons gluten free Sorghum Flour

½ cup + 2 tablespoons gluten free Potato Starch

3 tablespoons gluten free Potato Flour

½ teaspoon gluten free Guar Gum

1 teaspoon gluten free Baking Powder

Lady Kisses gluten free

Baci di Dama senza glutine

1/8 teaspoon Salt

Chocolate Filling:

3 ounces gluten free Chocolate, melted

Place the dry ingredients (almond flour, sorghum flour, baking powder, guar gum and salt) in a small bowl. Whisk together and place bowl aside.

In bowl of stand mixer, cut in 11 tablespoons of room temperature butter. Mix on medium high for a moment. On medium high, gradually add the sugar. Beat until light and fluffy. Beat in the egg and the almond extract.

Place mixer on low and gradually add the bowl of dry ingredients to the wet batter. You want to make sure the batter is evenly combined.

Place the dough in the refrigerator for at least 2 hours. I wrap the dough in plastic wrap and place in a lidded bowl and place in fridge to chill. The dough needs to chill so it can set. However, you don't want the dough to dry out. Be sure the batter is adequately covered so the dehydrating properties of the refrigeration process won't dry it out. If you leave it in the fridge overnight you can do so, but the dough must be retrieved and placed on the counter to warm up for at least 20 minutes before using.

I use a dough blade to cut off pieces, some people may prefer to break off pieces in their hands. Once you have a small piece in your hands roll in center of your palms to create small balls 1.5 inches in diameter.
The balls must be uniform in size if you plan to line up chocolate in center to create a cookie sandwich. 1.5" dough balls will yield 2" baked cookies.

Preheat oven to 350 degrees. Place aside an ungreased cookie sheet for the cookie dough to bake on. On a parchment paper lined cookie sheet, line up 1.5" dough balls approximately 2.5 inches apart. Flatten each ball slightly with center of palm to help cookie bake in a uniform roundness.

Bake in the center of a 350 degree pre-heated oven for 11 minutes on an ungreased cookie sheet. Remove from the oven. Leave on cookie sheet for 2 minutes (for cookie to set), then transfer to cooling rack.

This dough recipe yields 36 – 40 cookies. While the cookies are cooling or once cooled, prepare the melted chocolate. I know some people are into microwaving chocolate to melt it, but I swear it imparts an odd bitterness to the chocolate, not to mention the toxins associated with microwaving foods in plastic. Place some water in the bottom of a double boiler and place on low. Place broken and crumbled chocolate in top part of double boiler.

Allow chocolate to melt. If you are making cookie sandwiches this chocolate is ample for the drizzle the cookie will require. If you plan to just drizzle chocolate across the top of individual cookies, add a teaspoon of butter to the chocolate, to give the chocolate a rich satiny luster.

Assemble the cookie sandwiches: drizzle a bit of chocolate in the very center of the cookie, enough so that when you place the top cookie in position, it will push chocolate from the center out to the sides. Enough chocolate should be visible from the side to distinguish there is chocolate in the center, not enough for the cookies to begin sliding apart. Delicately balance cookie sandwiches on cooling rack until you are sure the chocolate is set and completely cooled.

Lady Kisses full gluten

These buttery and nutty cookies are delicious alone, drizzled with chocolate, or sandwiched with chocolate or a berry jam.

Yields Approximately 4 dozen individual cookies

Cookie Dough:

10 tablespoon Butter, room temperature

½ Confectioner's Sugar

1 Egg Yolk

½ teaspoon Almond Extract

1 cup Almond Meal

1 ½ cups all-purpose flour

Chocolate Glaze:

3 ounces Chocolate, melted

In bowl of stand mixer, cut in 11 tablespoons of room temperature butter. Mix on medium high for a moment. On medium high, gradually add the sugar. Beat until light and fluffy. Beat in the egg and the almond extract.

Place mixer on low and gradually add the bowl of dry ingredients to the wet batter. The batter should be evenly combined.

I use a dough blade to cut off pieces, some people may prefer to break off pieces in their hands. Once you have a small piece in your hands roll in center of your palms to create small balls 1.5 inches in diameter. The balls must be uniform in size if you plan to line up chocolate in center to create a cookie sandwich. 1.5" dough balls will yield 2" baked cookies.   Preheat oven to 350 degrees. These cookies have enough butter to not require additional oil. Place aside an ungreased cookie sheet for the cookie dough to bake on. On an ungreased cookie sheet, line up 1 1/2" dough balls approximately 2 1/2 inches apart. Flatten each ball slightly with center of palm to help cookie bake in a uniform roundness.

Bake in the center of a 350 degree pre-heated oven for 11 minutes on an ungreased cookie sheet. Remove from the oven. Leave on cookie sheet for 2 minutes (for cookie to set), then transfer to cooling rack. The dough recipe yields 36 – 40 cookies.

While the cookies are cooling or once cooled, prepare the melted chocolate. I know some people are into microwaving chocolate to melt it, but I swear it imparts an odd bitterness to the chocolate, not to mention the toxins associated with microwaving foods in plastic. Place some water in the bottom of a double boiler and place on low. Place broken and crumbled chocolate in top part of double boiler.

Allow chocolate to melt. If you are making cookie sandwiches this chocolate is ample for the drizzle the cookie will require. If you plan to drizzle chocolate across the top of individual cookies, add a teaspoon of butter to the chocolate, to give the chocolate a rich satiny luster.

Assemble Cookie Sandwiches: drizzle a bit of chocolate in the very center of the cookie, enough so that when you place the top cookie in position, it will push chocolate from the center out to the sides Delicately balance cookie sandwiches on cooling rack until the chocolate is set and completely cooled.

Crescent Cookies gluten free

Biscotti di Mezzaluna senza glutine

Crescent cookies are delicious butter cookies and packed with protein! Familiar and popular in many European cultures, in the US we usually see them during the holidays. What I love about these cookies is their taste. They lend themselves beautifully to a cup of coffee.

Some thoughts on how I came to choose the ingredients: butter provides a moisture base for this biscotti, I chose to not change the amount of butter for fear of making the cookie too greasy. The Sorghum flavor is reminiscent of wheat and its protein content helps provide structure; the use of two starches provides binding and Sorghum flavor is reminiscent of wheat. You will note the original full gluten recipe relies solely on the gluten as a rising agent.

Yields Approximately 4 ½ dozen

1 cup Butter, room temperature

¾ cup gluten free Confectioner's Sugar

1 teaspoon gluten free Vanilla Extract

1 cup Walnut meal, processed very fine

1 cup gluten free Sorghum Flour

½ cup gluten free Brown Rice Flour

¼ cup gluten free Arrowroot Starch

¼ cup gluten free Potato Starch

1 tablespoon gluten free Potato Flour

½ teaspoon gluten free Guar gum

1/3 -1/2 cup gluten free Confectioner's Sugar

Preheat the oven to 275 degrees. Either butter a cookie sheet or line with parchment paper.

Prepare and process the walnuts to a fine meal in a food processor.

Place all dry ingredients (including the walnut meal) in a small bowl, whisk to fully combine and place aside. Cream butter, add confectioner's sugar and continue to cream with butter until light and fluffy. Make sure to scrape down sides with a spatula.

Add vanilla. Gradually mix in the dry ingredients. With your hands, pluck pieces of batter about 1 ½ inches and shape into small barrel by rolling the plucked batter in the center of your palms. Then wrap around a finger to create the crescent bend. Place them about 2" apart from each other on cookie sheet.

Bake 35 minutes in the center rack of preheated oven, until just golden. Place ¼ cup of remaining confectioner's sugar in a shallow bowl for dusting cookies. Place aside. Leave on cookie sheet for 10 minutes once removed from oven. While the cookies are still warm, purge a cookie at a time in the confectioner's sugar on the top and bottom. Place on cooling rack.

Crescent Cookies *full gluten*

Yields approximately 4 ½ dozen

1 cup Butter, room temperature

¾ cup Confectioner's Sugar

1 teaspoon Vanilla Extract

2 cups sifted all-purpose flour

1 cup Walnut Meal

Preheat the oven to 275 degrees.

Either butter a cookie sheet or line with parchment paper.

Prepare and process the walnuts to a fine meal in a food processor.

Place all dry ingredients (including the walnut meal) in a small bowl, whisk to fully combine and place aside.

Cream butter, add confectioner's sugar and continue to cream with butter until light and fluffy. Make sure to scrape down sides with a spatula.

Add vanilla.

Gradually mix in the all-purpose flour followed by walnut meal. With your hands, pluck pieces of batter about 1 ½ inches and shape into small barrel by rolling the plucked batter in the center of your palms. Then wrap around one of your fingers to create the crescent bend. Place them about 2" apart from each other on cookie sheet.

Bake 35 minutes in the center rack of preheated oven, until just golden. Place ¼ cup of remaining confectioner's sugar in a shallow bowl for dusting cookies. Place aside.

Leave cookies on cookie sheet for 10 minutes once removed from oven. While the cookies are still warm, purge a cookie at a time in the confectioner's sugar on the top and bottom. Place on cooling rack.

Storing Crescent Cookies: Store cookies un-powdered in wax paper lined tin.

I don't use the cookie tin cover, I just use the waxed paper.

Panallets gluten free

Panallets are an amazing snack, loaded with protein; moist and sweet on the inside - crisp and nutty on the outside. It seems to me the original recipe was begging to be transformed to gluten free. There are so many nuts in this recipe! When it is a challenge to buy such an assortment of nuts, almonds alone are delicious.

Yields approximately 4 dozen

½ pound Sweet Potatoes, peeled and cut into chunks.

3 cups Almonds, finely chopped

1 cup White Sugar

¾ cup Light Brown Sugar

½ cup + 1 tablespoon gluten free Sorghum Flour

Panallets gluten free

¼ cup gluten free Brown Rice Flour

¼ cup gluten free Arrowroot Starch

2 Eggs, separated

1 tablespoon grated Lemon Zest

2 teaspoons gluten free Vanilla Extract

½ cup Pignoli (Pine nuts)

½ cup Hazelnuts, coarsely chopped

Boil the sweet potatoes for 15 minutes until cooked through. Drain, mash well, cool. Pre-heat oven to 350 degrees, butter two cookie sheets, or line with parchment. In a small bowl, combine the dry ingredients sorghum flour, brown rice flour and the arrowroot, whisk together and set aside.

Place potatoes in bottom of mixing bowl, add almond meal, sugar, dry ingredients, 2 egg yolks, the egg white, lemon zest and vanilla to potatoes, mix well. Using your hands, knead dough a few minutes until it holds together.

In shallow bowl, lightly beat egg whites. In another bowl stir together the pignoli and hazelnuts. To form each cookie, pinch of a piece of the dough the size of a walnut and roll it into a ball between palms. Flatten the ball a bit, brush it with egg white from one egg and roll it in the nut mixture, coating evenly. Place one inch apart on cookie sheet. Bake until golden, about 16 minutes. Allow to cool 2 minutes on cookie sheet before removing to wire rack.

Panallets full gluten

Panallets are incredibly scrumptious! The use of ingredients such as nut meals and sweet potato intrigued my curiosity to create the gluten free culinary cultural transformation which precedes this recipe.

½ pound Sweet Potatoes, peeled and cut into chunks.

3 cups Almonds, finely chopped

2 cups Sugar

½ cup all-purpose flour

2 Eggs, separated

1 tablespoon grated Lemon Zest

1 teaspoon Vanilla Extract

½ cup Pignoli (Pine nuts)

½ cup Hazelnuts, coarsely chopped

Boil the sweet potatoes for 15 minutes (until cooked through). Drain, mash well, cool. Pre-heat oven to 350 degrees, butter two cookie sheets, or line with parchment. Place potatoes in bottom of mixing bowl, add almond meal, sugar, flour, egg yolks, lemon zest and vanilla to potatoes and mix well.

Using your hands, knead dough a few minutes until it holds together. Cover with a kitchen towel and let rest about 30 minutes. In a shallow bowl, lightly beat egg whites. In another bowl stir together the pignoli and hazelnuts. To form each cookie, pinch of a piece of the dough the size of a walnut and roll it into a ball between palms. Flatten the ball a bit, brush it with egg whites and roll it in the nut mixture, coating evenly. Place one inch apart on cookie sheet. Bake until golden, about 15 minutes.

Genetti:

These cookies are where it all began for me. I was a very young teen when my favorite Auntie, Vincenza, passed away. Her son, John Anzalone, mentioned in passing conversation that he wished he had her Genetti recipe. Having had it, I told him I would write it down and mail it to him. I went home and searched my small file of handwritten recipes. To my dismay, the recipe was not there. I searched and searched, sometimes still do, looking for that little white piece of paper with my little girl handwriting. Although I was young, I instantly understood her recipe was gone and so was she. In that moment I grasped the importance of saving recipes since they are the nurturing memories of those who came before.

Genetti gluten free

Anise Serpent Cookies

I grew up making Genetti with my Great Aunties. An old world treasure, this recipe is one of those particular Southern Italian biscotti which begins with just a bit of moisture and gets dryer over time. Traditional in every way, they are a perfect accompaniment to Espresso or Café Americano.

These anise flavored serpent shaped cookies. Serpents are an ancient form to many lands throughout Europe and Southern Italy. They are a respected spirit creature from before Christian times. The Pre-Christian perspective looks at serpents, or snakes, as a symbol of wisdom and regeneration. These biscotti in serpent shape are a way of celebrating life during the darkness of winter.

When I was a child, I used to love working with this dough, rolling snakes was my specialty. I couldn't wait to become old enough to be allowed to form the serpent shape of the biscotti myself. I still love the feel of the dough underneath my skin, rolling the snake to the correct length and diameter without even thinking about it. The activity itself is a form of active meditation, allowing my thinking brain to wander away while I get into the rhythm of rolling. The act of being in the moment, not thinking about before or later is always a special gift during an otherwise crazy day.

This is the recipe which makes me feel like a girl. Just the act of hands well of flour brings comfort to my soul. I call it communing with my Ancestors.

Genetti gluten free

Yields 2 dozen

¼ cup gluten free Potato Flour

1/3 cup gluten free Potato Starch

2/3 cup gluten free White Rice Flour

¾ cup gluten free Sorghum Flour

2 ¼ teaspoons gluten free Baking Powder

¾ teaspoon gluten free Guar Gum

1/8 teaspoon Salt

6 tablespoons Sugar

1 cup (8 ounces) cold Butter

4 Whole Eggs

4 teaspoons gluten free Anise Extract

1 teaspoon gluten free Vanilla Extract

Sift all of the dry ingredients together in a large mixing bowl. Cube cold butter into smaller and manageable pieces. Using a pastry blender aerate the flour and whisk in sugar – one tablespoon at a time.

Using the pastry blender "cut" in the cold butter, a few pieces at a time. Blend and stomp with the blades, keep a butter knife on hand to periodically scrape batter of the tines of the blender. Do this until the flour is a pebbly texture.

Make a well in the flour. Add one egg, blend and combine thoroughly. Repeat this process until you have added all four eggs. Add the anise & vanilla extracts. Blend into batter following each teaspoon addition of flavor.

The texture should be sticky, but distinctly dough, not a thin batter. Shape the dough into a round. Cover in plastic wrap. Place in thick bowl in refrigerator for at least a half hour. I often allow as long as two hours before I get onto the next steps.

To assemble or create the serpent: Pre-heat the oven to 350 degrees. Butter a cookie sheet. Use a board specifically for gluten free dough. I dust it ever so slightly with starch. This is not wheat, using too much additional flour or starch will dry out the dough. Remember, gluten free flours tend to require more moisture than wheat, adding additional flour compromises the moisture balance. In baking, fats coat the proteins in flour - which water proofs them - making the protein strands slippery so the carbon dioxide gas bubbles can move easily. This lubrication makes dough more pliable.

Break off a two inch clump from the dough with your fingers. Roll the clump under your palm to get the air out and make the dough more pliable, then roll it around in a circular motion a few times.

Break the ball in half. Roll (spread) the ball under your fingers in a gentle motion to form a length about ½ inch wide by 5 inches long snake. Roll forward and gently spread your fingers apart to gently pull the dough and elongate. This action encourages protein bonds to stretch, it needs to be gentle and slow (slower than the reaction gluten rich flour has).

Hold the length (snake) in one hand. Using the other hand, twist in a slow circular motion to turn the length into a snake in a coiled up position. Use a light touch and don't over think it, after a few, you will get the hang of it. Place the coiled serpent cookies onto the buttered cookie sheet spaced about 2 inches apart. Bake for 12 minutes. Remove to cooling racks.

Genetti full gluten

5 cups All-Purpose Flour

8 teaspoons Baking Powder

1 1/3 cups Sugar

7 Eggs

8 tablespoons Butter, melted

2 teaspoons Vanilla Extract

3 teaspoons Sambuca

158   Kitchen Wisdom Gluten Free

Use a large bowl: Beat eggs, mix in sugar and temper in melted butter, followed by vanilla and Sambuca. Gradually add the flour, using the back of a wooden spoon to mix the flour into the batter. Continue to add the flour in this manner until all of it is absorbed.   Then knead the dough on a floured board for a couple of minutes to completely combine.

Break off a two inch clump from the dough with your fingers. Roll the clump under your palm to get the air out and make the dough more pliable. Just roll it around in a circular motion a few times.

Break the ball in half. Roll (spread) the ball under your fingers in a gentle motion to form a length about ½ inch wide by 5 inches long snake. Roll forward and gently spread your fingers apart to gently pull the dough and elongate. This action encourages protein bonds to stretch, it needs to be gentle and slow (slower than the reaction gluten rich flour has).

Hold the length (snake) in one hand. Using the other hand twist in a slow circular motion to turn the length into a snake in a coiled up position. Use a light touch and don't over think it, after a few, you will get the hang of it.

Place the coiled serpent cookies onto the buttered cookie sheet spaced about 2 inches apart. Bake for 12 minutes. Remove to cooling racks. Ice cookies when completely cool, using the recipe above.

Simple White Icing for Genetti gluten free

This simple white icing is used on countless cookies from Southern Italy & Sicily. This icing can also be host to a few drops of gluten free liqueur. The real role of the icing in this recipe is to seal in the cookie's moisture.

Yield icing for 2 Dozen Genetti

1 1/3 cups gluten free Confectioner's Sugar

8 teaspoons Milk

2 teaspoons gluten free Anise Extract

To avoid excess crumbs and to keep the icing fresh while I work, *I recommend making 2 separate batches.* The goal is to limit the amount of crumbs in the icing, smaller batches is one way of accomplishing this. I prefer a thicker icing, so I use 4 teaspoons of milk and 1 teaspoon of anise extract to 2/3 cup confectioner's sugar. If you prefer a thinner icing, more like a translucent glaze, then you will whisk in anywhere between ½ teaspoon – 1 ½ teaspoons of additional milk. Be sure to whisk in the additional milk ½ teaspoon at a time and whisk it smooth, lumps can be so unbecoming on a delicious biscotti.

In a small bowl that you can manage with one hand, vigorously whisk together 2/3 cup confectioner's sugar and add 1 teaspoon of anise extract, whisk thoroughly to coat sugar. Then add 2 teaspoons of milk, followed by 1 additional teaspoon of milk. Then add an additional teaspoon of milk and frantically whisk again, being sure to create a smooth icing. If the icing is too thin it will run loose and dry very clear.

Icing the cookies is not difficult, but it does require patience. I get into a Zen Kitchen moment and just keep moving, quiet the thinking brain and just become flow.

Create your Dipping Workstation: Place wax paper on counter, place empty cooling racks on top of wax paper. Place dipped cookies on rack to dry.

To Coat the Cookies: Tap off excess cookie crumbs at start, do this away from icing bowl. With icing bowl in one hand, and a face down cookie in the other, methodically dunk and twist the cookie in circular motion. Using a quick circular motion, gently dip the top of the cookie in the icing bowl, coating the entire surface of the cookie. Return cookie top side up, to a cooling rack on wax paper to dry. Try to avoid double dipping, as this usually gets crumbs in the icing. When your icing batch is done, if there are crumbs in the bowl, use a paper towel to remove excess crumb icing, and begin another batch.

"Cutting" Cold Butter into Recipes: Use a pastry blender to "cut" the butter into the flour, allowing the flour to coat the butter. The butter covers the individual strands of flour and protein bonds form. These bonds strengthen during baking. This is why delicate pastries often use cold butter.

Lemon Cookies gluten free
Biscotti di Lemon senza glutine

Lemon cookies rely on lemon extract, I add a bit of lemon zest in the dough to heighten the flavor on the palate. In lieu of generic extract add Limoncello to bring a delightful reward to the senses. This recipe is a good example of how extract changes everything, please refer to the Genetti recipe if looking for full gluten version.

¼ cup gluten free Potato Flour

1/3 cup gluten free Potato Starch

2/3 cup gluten free White Rice Flour

¾ cup gluten free Sorghum Flour

2 ¼ teaspoons gluten free Baking Powder

¾ teaspoon gluten free Guar Gum

1/8 teaspoon Salt

6 tablespoons Sugar

1 cup (8 ounces) cold Butter

4 Whole Eggs

2 teaspoon lemon zest

3 teaspoons gluten free Lemon Extract

Sift all of the dry ingredients together in a large mixing bowl.   Cube cold butter into smaller and manageable pieces. Using a pastry blender, aerate the flour and whisk in sugar, one tablespoon at a time. Then "cut" in the cold butter, a few pieces at a time. Blend and stomp with the blender, keep a butter knife on hand to periodically scrape batter off the tines of the blender. Do this until the flour is a pebbly texture.

Make a well in the flour. Add one egg, blend and combine thoroughly. Repeat this process until you have added all four eggs. Add lemon zest and lemon extract. Blend into batter with each teaspoon addition of flavor.

The texture should be sticky, but distinctly dough, not a thin batter. Shape the dough into a round. Cover in plastic wrap. Place in thick bowl in refrigerator for at least a half hour. I often allow as long as two hours before I get onto the next steps.

To assemble or create the serpent: Pre-heat the oven to 350 degrees. Butter a cookie sheet.

Gluten Free Biscotti di Limon Dough - use a board specifically for gluten free dough. I dust it ever so slightly with starch. This is not wheat, using too much additional flour or starch will dry out the dough. Remember, gluten free flours tend to require more moisture than wheat, adding additional flour compromises the moisture balance.

Break off a two inch clump from the dough with your fingers. Roll the clump under your palm to get the air out and make the dough more pliable. Just roll it around in a circular motion a few times.

Break the ball in half. Roll (spread) the ball under your fingers in a gentle motion to form a length about ½ inch wide by 5 inches long snake. Roll forward and gently spread your fingers apart to gently pull the dough and elongate. This action encourages protein bonds to stretch, it needs to be gentle and slow (slower than the reaction gluten rich flour has).

Hold the length (snake) in one hand. Using the other hand twist in a slow circular motion to turn the length into a snake in a coiled up position. Use a light touch and don't over think it, after a few, you will get the hang of it.

Place the coiled serpent cookies onto the buttered cookie sheet spaced about 2 inches apart. Bake for 12 minutes. Remove to cooling racks. Ice when completely cool.

Simple White Icing for Lemon Biscotti:

This icing is used on countless cookies from Southern Italy & Sicily. This icing can also be host to a few drops of gluten free liqueur. Its real role in this recipe is to seal in the cookie's moisture.

To coat 2 Dozen Biscotti di Limon:

1 1/3 cups gluten free Confectioner's Sugar

8 teaspoons Milk

2 teaspoons gluten free Lemon Extract

To avoid excess crumbs and to keep the icing fresh while I work, *I recommend making 2 separate batches*. The goal is to limit the amount of crumbs in the icing, smaller batches is one way of accomplishing this. I prefer a thicker icing, so I use 4 teaspoons of milk and 1 teaspoon of Anisette to 2/3 cup confectioner's sugar. If you prefer a thinner icing, more like a translucent glaze, then you will whisk in anywhere between ½ teaspoon – 1 ½ teaspoons of additional milk. Be sure to whisk in the additional milk ½ teaspoon at a time and whisk it smooth, lumps can be so unbecoming on a delicious biscotti.

In a small bowl that you can manage with one hand, vigorously whisk together 2/3 cup confectioner's sugar and add 1 teaspoon of Lemon Extract, whisk thoroughly to coat sugar. Then add 2 teaspoons of milk, followed by 1 additional teaspoon of milk. Then add an additional teaspoon of milk and frantically whisk again, being sure to create a smooth icing. If the icing is too thin it will run loose and dry very clear.

Icing the cookies is not difficult, but it does require patience. I get into a Zen Kitchen moment and just keep moving, quiet the thinking brain and just become flow.

Create your Dipping Workstation: Place wax paper on counter, place empty cooling racks on top of wax paper. Place dipped cookies on rack to dry.

To Coat the Cookies: Tap off excess cookie crumbs at start, do this away from icing bowl. With icing bowl in one hand, and a face down cookie in the other, methodically dunk and twist the cookie in circular motion. Using a quick circular motion, gently dip the top of the cookie in the icing bowl, coating the entire surface of the cookie. Return cookie top side up, to a cooling rack on wax paper to dry. Try to avoid double dipping, as this usually gets crumbs in the icing. When your icing batch is done, if there are crumbs in the bowl, use a paper towel to remove excess crumb icing, and begin another batch.

Dorothea's Filled Cookies gluten free

I present my cousin Dorothea Demari's yummy Italian bakery style cookies. Their full gluten counterparts are rolled dough. To convert this recipe to something thoroughly delicious and most closely resembling the original in flavor, I chose not to make gluten free rolling dough; this recipe is more of a thick batter.

Yields approximately 2 dozen

½ cup Butter (room temperature)

4 Whole Eggs

¾ cup Sugar

2/3 cup gluten free Sorghum Flour

¼ cup gluten free Potato Flour

2/3 cup gluten free White Rice Flour

1/3 cup gluten free Potato Starch

1 teaspoon gluten free Guar Gum

2 teaspoons gluten free Baking Powder

1/8 teaspoon Salt

Sift dry ingredients (sorghum, potato flour and starch, white rice flour, guar gum, baking powder, salt) into a mixing bowl.

Mix sugar into dry ingredients.

Cube room temperature butter, gradually mix butter into dry ingredients.

Add one egg at a time, mixing batter in between each addition. Scrape down batter from sides of bowl after each egg addition.

Refrigerate batter for one hour.

Preheat oven to 375 degrees. Butter a cookie sheet.

Pluck ½ inch clumps of dough in fingers. Make a ball between palms and then place on cookie sheet. Pinch into diamond shape, use thumb to press down center of cookie.

If using prepared jam as filling: add ½ teaspoon of prepared raspberry or strawberry jam to center of cookies.

Bake 9-10 minutes, until golden.

Remove from oven, then remove cookies to wire racks to cool.

If filling with chocolate ganache, wait until cookies are completely cool before filling. Then cool completely again, once chocolate is added.

Store in bakery box lined with parchment or waxed paper. They keep for 7 days.

Dorothea's Filled Cookies full gluten

This recipe is courtesy of my cousin, Dorothea Demari. Because these are made with full gluten all-purpose flour, the dough from this recipe can be rolled, shaped and filled. This is the traditional way to prepare these cookies. This recipe heavily relies on eggs and gluten in the white wheat flour to form structure and give these biscotti their physical integrity.

Yields Approximately 2 dozen

1 cup Butter – room temperature (2 sticks, cubed)

6 Whole Eggs (beaten)

1 ½ cup Sugar

6 teaspoons Baking Powder

6 cups All-Purpose White Wheat Flour

Pinch Salt

1 whole egg, beaten for egg wash

Preheat oven to 375 degrees. Butter a cookie sheet, place aside.

In a large mixing bowl, make a well with the flour, baking powder and salt. In a small separate bowl beat 6 whole eggs, place aside. Beat 1 egg in small bowl for egg wash, set aside.

In the center of the well add the butter, sugar and eggs. Using your hands, combine and knead all of the ingredients until the dough is soft and pliable.

Pluck small amounts of dough and using a rolling pin, roll out into long strips: 8"x 4" wide. Place filling over the middle of the strip, takes sides and cover over filling.

Brush with egg wash. Bake for 12-15 minutes, until golden brown. Remove to wire racks to cool. Once completely cooled, cut cookies into strips. Store them in bakery box with parchment or waxed paper.

Fillings

Prepared Jam Filling naturally gluten free

Use store bought or home-made raspberry or strawberry jam; spoon onto uncooked cookie by ½ teaspoon full.

Traditional Jam Filling naturally gluten free

This is a bit more elaborate in taste than using prepared jam alone. For the jam use raspberry, strawberry, apricot or fig jam or preserves.

4   teaspoon Prepared Jam or Preserves (raspberry, strawberry, apricot or fig)

1 teaspoon finely chopped Nuts (walnut, almonds or hazelnuts) – (optional)

finely chopped gluten free Chocolate shavings (optional)

¼ teaspoon Cinnamon

1 tablespoon Orange Juice

Combine all in bowl, whisk together.

Prepare before beginning cookies, so the flavors have time to marry.

Add ¼ - ½ teaspoon to uncooked Italian bakery cookie recipes.

Chocolate Filling gluten free

5 tablespoons gluten free Chocolate Chips

1 teaspoon Butter

Splash Heavy Cream or Half and Half

Double Boiler

Place some water in bottom of double boiler, bring to rolling simmer.

Place butter and chocolate chips in top of double boiler. Once melted, add a splash of cream and whisk together. Place ½ teaspoon of melted chocolate as filling in center of cookies after fully baked.

When chocolate is added, allow cookie to cool completely again. Place any leftover chocolate in container. Cool and place in fridge. Chocolate filling will keep for a few weeks in fridge. Reheat in top of warmed double boiler.

Chocolate for Melting: Chocolate usually contains hidden gluten because it is usually made with either barley malt or the emulsifier soy lecithin. Soy grown in the US, at the time of this writing, is almost always cross contaminated with wheat (gluten). It is very important for people with gluten issues to eat gluten free chocolate. Barley is a gluten containing grain and therefore unsafe. Read the nutrition statement and contact the manufacturer if necessary.

Savory Pepper "Cakes" gluten free

Pepper "Cakes" are a wonderful savory snack. I grew up with these from bakeries in various neighborhoods. Very spicy, sometimes called pepper biscuits or biscotti di pepe, they can be found in different versions in Italian bakeries, bread bakeries, pasta markets and pork stores. Once in a while a relation or friend would make these from scratch. These really are tastier from scratch. They make a quick carb with a salad, also delicious with a soup or stew. They are equally as delicious in a snack bag in your desk or purse.

As far as I can tell, the truly amazing and versatile wheat grain has an Achilles tendon. When used for small baked items, if not leavened properly the product can become quite dense. Wheat seems to need yeast for minor lifting action. The original recipe calls for yeast. When converting this recipe I chose to rely on the eggs in combination with baking powder and guar gum as leaven and added milk to improve the protein content and provide moisture and richer flavor. I also included unflavored gelatin to support the overall structure.

Yields 2 dozen

2/3 cup gluten free Sorghum Flour

2/3 cup gluten free Brown Rice Flour

2/3 cup gluten free Potato Starch

1 tablespoon gluten free Baking Powder

½ teaspoon gluten free Guar Gum

1 packet gluten free Unflavored Gelatin

Savory Pepper "Cakes" gluten free

Biscotti Di Pepe   senza glutine

1 ¾ teaspoon Pepper (more or less for personal taste)

½ teaspoon Salt

1 whole Egg

1 Egg Yolk

½ cup + 3 tablespoons Milk

Olive Oil (enough to oil cookie sheet)

Take out milk and eggs. Place aside, allow to become tepid or room temp. Beat whole egg and egg yolk in small bowl, place aside. Combine dry ingredients in mixing bowl. Mix. Gradually add egg, mix until well combined.

   Place dough in the refrigerator for 30 minutes. 15 minutes before dough is ready turn on oven to 375 degrees. Using olive oil, oil the cookie sheet and place aside.

Grease a cookie sheet with olive oil. Pluck 1" x 2" clumps from dough. Squeeze and roll dough between palms. Form barrel or loaf shape 1 ½ " - 2" long by ¾ " – 1" diameter. Place on cookie sheet 1" – 1 ½" apart. Bake 20 minutes, transfer to wire racks. Cool completely. *Storage:* line the bottom of a paper bag with a bit of parchment or wax paper. Place biscuits in bag. Roll top of bag down. These will keep for many days on counter or in cabinet this way. For those who like it HOT: I like it hot – do you like it hot? Add some hot crushed red pepper for heat.

Savory Pepper "Cakes" full gluten

Yields 2 dozen

2 cups All-Purpose Flour

1 tablespoon of Yeast

¼ cup warm water

½ teaspoon Salt

1 teaspoon Pepper

Whisk together and fully combine flour, pepper and salt in a large bowl. Put yeast in warm water. Once the yeasts react, gradually pour the water into the flour mixture.   Once all of the water is poured in, knead mixture into a ball.

Place in an oiled bowl, cover with plastic wrap and leave somewhere warm to rise for about 25 minutes. Once the dough has risen, punch down again, cover and let rise again until double in size. Pre-heat the oven to 375 degrees

. Flour a board, roll out dough and cut into ¼ inch long strips. Cut strips into 2 inch pieces, ½ inch in diameter. Lay out on ungreased cookie sheet. Bake 15 minutes. If you prefer a super dry pepper cake, lower the oven to 200 degrees and leave pepper cakes to dry out for a couple of hours.

Cake & Cheescake

Torte e Torte di Formaggio

I have chosen to include the traditional gluten rich recipes, in the cookies and cakes chapters, to serve a twofold purpose. As a learning tool, I find the original recipe very helpful. When I transform recipes to gluten free I observe a number of things concerning the gluten rich flour. For example, I look at the ratio of gluten rich flour to moisture. I also look for fat content in relation to the total amount of gluten rich flour. I believe the inclusion of the original gluten rich recipes is important for those of us who learned to bake using gluten rich flour. Additionally, the inclusion of the original gluten rich recipes is my part of preservation of the culinary culture I was raised with. Their inclusion is part of a grand international movement of cultural preservation, particular to the Province of Caserta in the Campania Region of Italy. For more information, please visit Chapter One "Culinary Cultural Evolution."

How can I speak about baking without speaking about my Zia Vincenza? She was so influential in my world as a child. She baked in the old world method, nothing electric. Turning the batter with a wooden spoon was often my responsibility. She would softly add ingredient after ingredient, and I would stir. She was methodical. At the final stage of batter she would then take the bowl and with a magical hand show me how to pass one more swoop along the side and the very bottom with the spoon, thus making sure all of the batter from high on the sides and deep in the belly of the bowl would be used. She would say "baking is all about when and how wet is added to dry or dry is added to wet"; and would illustrate the differences various baked goods have based on this principle. She always said that the difference begins with the timing of combining wet and dry ingredients. Timing, what an important lesson in life? When to act, when to not act. In many ways, life is all about timing and the addition or subtraction of circumstances in our lives.

Chocolate Espresso Cake gluten free

Torta di Cioccolato Espresso senza glutine

   Excellent with coffee, I chose to create the gluten free recipe with added leaven. The traditional recipe relies solely on eggs as the leavener to boost the gluten rich flour. The eggs provide protein, moisture and structure to baked goods. Because gluten free flours are weak they rely on additional leavener. Therefore, leavener must be added for conversion. I also chose to reduce the flour, thereby increasing the egg ratio.

¾ cup gluten free Sorghum flour

½ cup gluten free Brown Rice Flour

2 tablespoons gluten free Potato Starch

2 tablespoons gluten free Potato Flour

3 tablespoons Instant Espresso

½ cup gluten free Cocoa

2 teaspoon gluten free Baking Powder

1 teaspoon gluten free Guar Gum

1/8 teaspoon Salt

1 cup Butter (2 sticks) room temp

½ cup Sugar

4 whole Eggs

¾ cup Milk

Preheat oven to 350 degrees. Butter a 10 inch Bundt pan, set aside.   Combine dry ingredients (sorghum, brown rice flour, potato starch, potato flour cocoa, Leaveners, espresso, salt) and whisk in bowl – set aside. In bowl of mixer – cream together butter and sugar. Beat in one whole egg at a time. Mix and scrape down sides in between egg additions.

   Add dry to wet in mixing bowl in the following way: alternate dry and milk additions in two parts each. Be sure to aerate and scrape down batter from sides of bowl in between alternating additions.

   Place batter in loaf pan.   Bake in center of over 27-30 minutes. Insert knife or baking pick, cake is done when inserted comes out moist but clean. *Completely cool:* Serve with a sprinkling of fresh powdered sugar. Wrap air tight and store in fridge after initial serving. If you would like to serve with a chocolate glaze as pictured, please refer to below "Chocolate Topping."

Chocolate Espresso Cake full gluten

This traditional recipe relies solely on eggs as the leavener to boost the gluten rich flour. The eggs provide protein, moisture and structure to baked goods. I hope you enjoy the following full gluten recipe. It really is quick, easy and tasty!

2 cups All-Purpose Flour

½ cup Cocoa

3 tablespoons Instant Espresso

1 cup Butter (2 sticks) room temp

½ cup sugar

5 whole Eggs

Preheat oven to 350 degrees. Butter a a 10 inch Bundt pan, set aside. Combine dry ingredients (flour, cocoa, espresso) and whisk in bowl – set aside. In bowl of mixer – cream together butter and sugar. Beat in one whole egg at a time. Mix and scrape down sides in between egg additions.

Add dry to wet in mixing bowl in the following way: alternate dry and milk additions in two parts each. Be sure to aerate and scrape down batter from sides of bowl in between alternating additions.

Place batter in buttered loaf pan. Bake in center of over 25-27 minutes. Insert knife or baking pick, cake is done when inserted comes out moist but clean.

Completely cool: Serve with a sprinkling of fresh powdered sugar. Wrap air tight and store in fridge after initial serving. If you would like to serve with a chocolate glaze as pictured, please refer to below "Chocolate Glaze."

Chocolate Glaze

Southern Italian baked goods are made with considerably less sugar than American baked goods. In my desire to stay close to the original recipe, I chose to not increase the sugar. To supplement the American palate, I sometimes serve this cake with a quick chocolate ganache like icing. I usually have chocolate chips in the cupboard. I place a pat of butter in the top of a pre-warmed double boiler. Add some chips - allow melting; once melted, add some cream to the mixture and whisk well till combined and drippy. I then drizzle the chocolate icing across the top of the cake. Allow to cool completely. You can also sprinkle some confectioner's sugar.

Espresso in Baking: Espresso provides boldness of flavor to chocolate in baked goods. Generally, Americans refer to this flavor as *Mocha*. You can see the original recipe calls for instant espresso. For those who keep espresso in the kitchen there is no need to purchase instant: place 2 ½ tablespoons of espresso in a spice mill and grind until the espresso is powder. This process yields approximately 3 tablespoons. The finished product functions as the instant espresso would during baking.

Nana's Chocolate Cake gluten free

This chocolate cake is a delicious recipe from my nana, my maternal grandmother (Yolanda Ruggiero). The cake is very moist and most delicious with frosting. The secret to a moist baked gluten free good is to be sure there is ample moisture in the batter. Gluten free flours absorb far more moisture than wheat. When transforming a recipe to gluten free, look to use additional moisture in combination with increasing protein. Milk, eggs, butter are all examples of increasing moisture in a baked good.

½ cup Butter (room temperature)

2 cups Sugar

4 Egg Yolks

6 ounces gluten free Bitter-Sweet or Semi-Sweet Chocolate

1 ½ teaspoon gluten free Vanilla Extract

1 ½ cups gluten free Sorghum Flour

2 tablespoons gluten free Potato Starch

¾ cups gluten free Brown Rice Flour

5 ¼ teaspoon gluten free Baking Powder

2 ¼ teaspoon gluten free Guar Gum

½ teaspoon Salt

1 ½ cups Milk (room temperature)

5 Egg Whites

¼ teaspoon gluten free Cream of Tartar

Preheat the oven to 300 degrees and butter and flour an 8 inch round cake pan. Place water in bottom of double boiler and place on low flame. Combine in a bowl and whisk together sorghum flour, potato starch, brown rice flour, baking powder, guar gum and salt.

Break up and crumble 6 ounces of bitter sweet chocolate into top of double boiler. On low, melt chocolate slowly. Using the bowl of a stand mixer (or using a hand mixer) beat butter for a few seconds till whipped. Gradually add sugar and continue to beat on medium high. Continue beating batter; add one egg yolk at a time, allowing egg to combine thoroughly. Put egg whites in small bowl and leave aside. The batter will be light, next add vanilla extract.

Once chocolate is melted, temper chocolate into batter. Place mixer on low. Gradually add dry ingredients to the wet batter, alternating with ½ cup additions of the milk (totaling 1 ½ cups). Alternate dry ingredients and milk addition in thirds. Allow batter to completely blend ingredients before the addition of the alternating ingredient. Scrape down sides of the bowl before adding final splash of milk.

In a separate bowl - beat egg whites until stiff peaks form. Add cream of tartar to egg whites before placing mixer on high. Gently fold egg white into batter. Place batter in buttered cake pan and bake for 40-45 minutes until a cake tester inserted in center of cake comes out clean. Cool completely before frosting. See frosting recipes that follow.

Nana's Chocolate Cake full gluten

½ cup Butter

1 ½ cups Sugar

4 Eggs, separated

4 ounces Bitter-Sweet or Semi-Sweet Chocolate

1 teaspoon Vanilla Extract

2 ½ cups All-Purpose flour

3 ½ teaspoons Baking Powder

1 ½ cups Milk

Preheat the oven to 300 degrees and butter and flour an 8inch round cake pan. Place water in bottom of double boiler and place on low flame. Sift the flour and baking powder into a small bowl. Place aside. Break up and crumble 6 ounces of chocolate into top of double boiler. On low, melt chocolate slowly.

Using the bowl of a stand mixer (or using a hand mixer) beat butter for a few seconds till whipped. Gradually add sugar and continue to beat on medium high. Continue to beat the batter, add one egg yolk at a time, allowing egg to combine thoroughly. Place egg white aside in small bowl for later. Batter will be light.

Add vanilla extract.

Once chocolate is melted, temper it into batter in a slow drizzle while mixing the batter.

Place mixer on low. Gradually add dry ingredients to the wet batter, alternating with ½ cup additions of the milk (totaling 1 ½ cups). Alternate dry ingredients and milk addition in thirds. Allow batter to completely blend ingredients before the addition of the alternating ingredient. Scrape down sides of the bowl before adding final splash of milk.

In a separate bowl - beat egg whites until stiff peaks form. Add cream of tartar to egg whites before placing mixer on high. Gently fold egg whites into batter.

Place in cake pan and bake for 40-45 minutes until a cake tester inserted in center of cake comes out clean. Cool completely before frosting. See below for frosting recipes.

Frosting

I learned all of the following from my grandmother (Yolanda Ruggiero). Using a hand mixer with a steady hand, mixing the ingredients while my grandmother added them was often my responsibility as a child.

Quick Buttercream Frosting gluten free

7 tablespoons Butter (room temperature)

2 cups Gluten Free Confectioner's Sugar (Confectioner's Sugar)

3 tablespoons - ¼ cup Milk (room temperature)

2 teaspoon gluten free Vanilla Extract

Add vanilla to milk and leave aside.   Whip the butter in bowl of stand mixer. Gradually add powdered sugar. Gradually add powdered sugar; alternate adding sugar with milk and vanilla mixture.   Frost cake when it has completely cooled.

Quick Chocolate Buttercream Frosting gluten free

3 tablespoons melted gluten free Chocolate

¼ cup Butter (room temperature)

3 cups gluten free Confectioner's Sugar

1 tablespoon Milk (room temperature)

Place double boiler on stove on low. Break up and crumble 3 ounces chocolate and place in top of double boiler. Allow chocolate to thoroughly melt. Cool slightly.

   Pour chocolate into bowl of stand mixer.   Add the room temperature butter one tablespoon at a time. Beat on medium low.

   Once chocolate and butter are creamed, gradually mix in the confectioner's sugar.   Add 1 tablespoon of milk to finish off frosting.

Chocolate Ricotta Frosting gluten free

5 tablespoons Ricotta (room temperature)

3 ounces melted gluten free Chocolate

3 cups gluten free Confectioner's Sugar

1 tablespoon gluten free Extract Vanilla

Place double boiler on stove on low. Break up and crumble 3 ounces chocolate and place in top of double boiler. Allow chocolate to thoroughly melt. Cool slightly.

Pour chocolate into bowl of stand mixer.

Add the room temperature ricotta one tablespoon at a time. Beat on medium low.

Once chocolate and ricotta are creamed, gradually mix in the confectioner's sugar.

Add 1 tablespoon of extract to finish off the frosting.

Orange Flower Water is also called Orange Blossom Water: Often a "secret" ingredient in many Italian pastries and desserts, it imparts a mild orange essence. It is a clear distillation of bitter orange blossoms. Purchase orange flower water at Italian or French specialty stores and many natural foods stores.

Zucchini Bread gluten free

This Gluten Free version of the classic Zucchini bread has a rich and moist crumb, warm flavor, an enticing delight. Remember when increasing eggs, the butter must be increased as well. The additional eggs provide structure and moisture. Potato Flour, which is different from potato starch, helps to keep baked goods moist. Therefore the smallest addition used in combination with other gluten free flours delivers a powerfully moist result.

Makes 1 Loaf

3 Eggs

1 Egg White

1 cup Sugar

1 ½ teaspoon gluten free Vanilla Extract

¾ cup Butter, melted

1 ½ cups grated Zucchini

½ cup + 2 tablespoons gluten free Sorghum Flour

½ cup + 1 tablespoon gluten free Brown Rice Flour

¼ cup gluten free Arrowroot Flour

1 tablespoon gluten free Potato Flour

½ cup Walnut Meal

1 teaspoon gluten free Baking Soda

1 teaspoon gluten free Baking Powder

¾ teaspoon gluten free Guar Gum

½ teaspoon Salt

1 teaspoon Cinnamon

1 tablespoon Lemon Zest

Pre-heat the oven to 350 degrees. Butter the inside of a loaf pan. In a separate bowl, combine the sorghum, brown rice flour, arrowroot, potato flour, walnut meal, baking soda, baking powder, guar gum, cinnamon and salt. Place aside.

Grate the zucchini, I recommend processing zucchini in a food processor using the grating blade.

In a mixing bowl beat the egg and egg white with the sugar until fluffy. Temper the melted butter into the egg and sugar batter by slowly drizzle the butter in while mixing the batter. Thoroughly combine. Add the vanilla extract and lemon zest. Thoroughly combine. Don't over mix, as this can make batter to heavy. Add the grated zucchini. Mix thoroughly. Pour into buttered loaf pan.

Bake in center of oven for one hour. Allow to cool before serving. Store overnight with wax paper and foil on top, then move into fridge.

Zucchini Bread full gluten

This is wonderful sweet loaf dessert bread. Great to make when zucchini is abundant. The smell while baking whispers autumn!

Makes 1 Loaf

1 Egg

1 Egg White

1 cup Sugar

1 ½ teaspoons Vanilla Extract

½ cup Butter, melted

1 ½ cups grated Zucchini

1 ½ cups All-Purpose flour

½ cup finely chopped Walnuts

½ teaspoon Baking Soda

½ teaspoon Baking Powder

½ teaspoon Salt

1 teaspoon Cinnamon

1 tablespoon Lemon Zest

Pre-heat the oven to 350 degrees. Butter the inside of a loaf pan.

In a separate bowl, combine the flour, walnut meal, baking soda, baking powder, cinnamon and salt. Place aside.

Grate the zucchini, I recommend processing zucchini in a food processor using the grating blade.

In a mixing bowl beat the egg and egg white with the sugar until fluffy.

Temper the melted butter into the egg and sugar batter by slowly drizzle the butter in while mixing the batter. Thoroughly combine.

Add the vanilla extract and lemon zest. Thoroughly combine. Don't over mix, as this can make batter to heavy. Add the grated zucchini. Mix thoroughly. Pour into buttered loaf pan.

Bake in center of oven for one hour. Allow to cool before serving. Store overnight with wax paper and foil on top, then move into fridge.

Cheesecake

Cheesecakes must be well mixed, but not over beaten.   It is important to not overcook or over mix the cheese in cheesecake. If there is too much air, the cake will puff up like soufflé in baking, then drop and crack when cool. Overbeating will create a thin and dense cake. If using a mixer, use the paddle attachment for the best texture. Always bake in moderate to low heat; many cakes do very well baking in a water bath (Bain-Marie). See below for more information on water baths.

Cannoli Cheesecake gluten free

I am pleased to present the gluten free makeover "Cannoli Cheesecake". What a great fusion recipe; many countless Italian cheesecakes use Ricotta as the cheese, the American addition of a graham cracker crust and chocolate chips at the top are just delightful and yummy!

This gluten free transformation has a few changes from the original gluten rich below. As a child my maternal grandmother often enlisted my help in the kitchen when making cannoli. I decided to go through some family cannoli creme recipes; in addition to orange zest I chose to use Orange Flower (Blossom) Water in place of some of the vanilla from the original recipe. I also use less sugar, this combination really kicks up the cannoli flavor.

During preparation to transform this recipe I sat with the idea that cheesecake is really an egg custard. Cheesecakes are sensitive and can require more attention than the average baked good. I chose to lower the heat to 325 from 350 degrees, this helps to reduce incidence of cracks and dryness. Dryness is especially important as gluten free flours tend to need more moisture than wheat. I also chose to use an 8" spring form pan and adjusted the original recipe accordingly. A hot water bath helps to maintain moisture level in the cake as it bakes. The steam helps the custard to slowly cook and then set. The cheesecake is done baking when the center just begins to set. Boil water and pour scalding water in a large roasting pan with rack in center if necessary. The cheesecake spring form pan needs to have double or triple layers with foil at its bottom – sealing out the water. Then the spring form with filling is placed in the center roasting pan. Place on rack in roasting pan if the roasting pan sides are taller than the spring form pan. Watch the water level in the roasting pan and keep boiling water on stove to add periodically to hot water bath.

You must use a high quality ricotta which also states on the container that it is a "smooth" or "creamier" type of ricotta. Ricotta that is low quality has no flavor and is not worth the money. When making this batter, be sure not to over mix it. Over mixing creates air pockets which creates a pastier flavor and makes the cake more likely to crack. The original recipe calls for just a bit of flour. The addition of gluten rich flour provides structure and binding for the ingredients. I chose to use a combination of potato starch for binding and sorghum flour for flavor and just a bit of bulk. I use prepackaged gluten free "graham" crackers and processed them in food processor, the old school bag and rolling pin method also works well and is always a great job for a youngster in the kitchen. I present the cook time for my oven, but remember cook times vary oven to oven, so just keep an eye out.

This cheesecake is worth all of the effort. When serving, I recommend placing a non-serrated cake cutter or cake knife in a glass of cold water, then slice cheesecake; this method makes slicing cheesecakes much easier.

Crust:

1 ½ cups gluten free "Graham" crackers

2 tablespoons Sugar

¼ cup melted Butter

Filling:

2 ½ pounds Ricotta

1 cup Sugar

¼ cup Potato Starch

2 tablespoons gluten free Sorghum Flour

2 teaspoons gluten free Orange Flower Water

2 teaspoons Orange Zest

2 teaspoons gluten free Vanilla Extract

5 whole Eggs

1/3 cup gluten free Semi-Sweet Chocolate Chips

Take Ricotta and eggs out of fridge to warm up to room temperature. Preheat oven to 350 degrees. Use an 8" spring form pan, butter inside and layer outside bottom of pan with 2 or 3 layers of foil. Retrieve a large roasting pan, fit with rack in center if pan is taller on sides than spring form pan. Place a large pot or kettle of water to boil on stove, when it boils adds water to roasting pan.

To make the "Graham" cracker Crust: I purchase gluten free "graham" crackers for this recipe. Melt butter, process gluten free "graham" crackers to crumbs in a food processor. Place crumbs in a small bowl, with fork toss in sugar, mix thoroughly. Gradually pour in melted butter while tossing with fork.

Assemble "Graham" cracker Crust: These layers need to be water tight. Dump the crumbs into the spring form pan and use your hand to press crumbs down into place at the bottom. Continue to press crumbs with your hands traveling about halfway up the inner side of the pan. Place crust in pre-heated oven, bake for 10minutes. Remove and allow to completely cool.

Reduce heat to 325 degrees. Place potato starch and sorghum in a small bowl and whisk together, place aside. Zest a small orange, place the zest aside. Beat 5 eggs in a small bowl and place aside. Prepare the Filling: In a large mixing bowl, cream together the ricotta and the sugar. Mix in the gluten free flours. Fold in the extracts and the orange zest. Gently fold in the beaten egg in three batches.   Add the filling to the completely cooled "graham" crusted spring form pan. Smooth top if necessary with spatula.

Place roasting pan with water (and rack if necessary) in center of pre-heated oven. Carefully place cheesecake in center of water bath. Close door. Watch water level and for browning or cracking on top.

Bake for 70-75 minutes, center of cake will be a bit jiggly and just set. Remove to wire rack to cool. After about a half hour, use a baker's knife to gentle pull cake from sides of spring form pan. Allow to cool completely (a few hours) before very gently removing spring form circle. Enjoy!

Cannoli Cheesecake full gluten

For detailed additional information on proper baking of a cheesecake please see above Cannoli Cheesecake gluten free recipe.

Crust:

1 ½ cups Graham crackers

2 tablespoons Sugar

¼ cup melted Butter

Filling:

2 ½ pounds Ricotta

1 cup Sugar

¼ cup Corn Starch

2 tablespoons All-Purpose Flour

2 teaspoons Orange Flower Water

2 teaspoons Orange Zest

1 teaspoon Vanilla Extract

5 whole Eggs

1/3 cup Semi-Sweet Chocolate Chips

Take Ricotta and eggs out of fridge to warm up to room temperature. Preheat oven to 350 degrees. Use an 8" spring form pan, butter inside and layer outside bottom of pan with 2 or 3 layers of foil. Retrieve a large roasting pan, fit with rack in center if pan is taller on sides than spring form pan. Place a large pot or kettle of water to boil on stove and bring to boil then add water to roasting pan.

To make the Crust: Melt butter, process gluten free "graham" crackers to crumbs in a food processor. Place crumbs in a small bowl, with fork toss in sugar, mix thoroughly. Gradually pour in melted butter while tossing with fork.

Assemble Crust: These layers need to be water tight. Dump crumbs into spring form pan, use your hand to press crumbs down into place at the bottom and traveling about halfway up the inner side of the pan.

Place crust in pre-heated oven, bake for 10minutes. Remove and allow to completely cool. Reduce heat to 325 degrees. Place potato starch and sorghum in a small bowl and whisk together, place aside. Zest a small orange, place the zest aside. Beat 5 eggs in a small bowl and place aside. Prepare the Filling: In a large mixing bowl, cream together the ricotta and the sugar. Mix in the gluten free flours. Fold in the extracts and the orange zest. Gently fold in the beaten egg in three batches.   Add the filling to the completely cooled "graham" crusted spring form pan. Smooth top if necessary with spatula.

Place roasting pan with water (and rack if necessary) in center of pre-heated oven. Carefully place cheesecake in center of water bath. Close door. Watch water level and for browning or cracking on top.

Bake for 70-75 minutes, center of cake will be a bit jiggly and just set. Remove to wire rack to cool. After about a half hour, use a baker's knife to gentle pull cake from sides of spring form pan. Allow to cool completely (a few hours) before very gently removing spring form circle. Enjoy!

Cheesecake Water bath (Bain-Marie): A water bath keeps the cheesecake moist by managing the heat during baking. *To Prepare Water Bath*: If you are using a spring form pan, place a double or triple layer of aluminum foil fitted to the outside of the pan to avoid water entering the bottom of the cake during baking. Place the cheesecake batter, which is actually custard, in a baking pan. The outside of the pan should sit partially in water.

Create a bath: Use a deep roasting pan, fitted with a rack. Use scalding water. Place the pan in the center of a pre-heated oven. Place the custard in the center of the pan. During baking, water evaporates, add more as needed. I keep a kettle of water on the stovetop during baking; the spout makes it easy to pour.

Baked Crema Pasticcera gluten free

Ordinarily this is a pastry creme, which works well inside of any sort of pastry shell, or served as a pudding. This recipe is somewhat unique in that it is baked and does not use flour. I don't recall where in my travels, whose particular kitchen it was that shared this version with me. I do know this custard was shared with me during Easter season, as one of the traditional recipes for that particular family. This recipe is so delicious I felt it needed to be shared, especially since it is gluten free. I learned this recipe using a more traditional method of whisking using a balloon whisk and bowl, I prefer my stand mixer.

This is a double recipe:

8 Whole Eggs, room temperature

¾ cup Sugar

2 ½ teaspoon gluten free Vanilla Extract

4 cups Whole Milk

Preheat oven to 325 degrees. Place rack in center of oven. Gather 2 pie dishes or medium shallow bowls, approximately 7-9 inches in diameter. Prepare a water bath see "Cook's Note" below.

Butter a piece of aluminum foil large enough to loosely cover entire pan with water and baking dishes. Leave aside.

In the top of a double boiler, warm the milk to hot just before skin forms (if it does form a skin, remove skin and remove from heat). Turn off, place aside. Using a stand mixer, or a bowl and large balloon whisk, whip eggs. Continue whisking and gradually add sugar, followed by vanilla. Temper the milk into the eggs (gradually whisk in a very small stream of hot milk to the egg mixture, the thin and slow stream). Continue to gradually pour the milk while whisking the egg milk mixture.

Pour the mixture into the two baking dishes. Place dishes on a rack inside of roast pan for water bath and place in pre-heated oven in center on rack.

Pour boiling or scalding water in pan, enough to cover two-thirds of the outer diameter of the baking dishes. Loosely cover with buttered aluminum foil, to prohibit thick skin formation. Bake 45-60 minutes.

The center must be quivery when baking dish is slightly shaken. If the center is completely firm, then the outer portion will be completely overcooked (and dry). To check, you can tilt dish slightly to a 45 degree angle, the center should remain firmly in place without overflowing.

Insert a cake tester one third of the way from the outer rim, toward the center. The tester should come out clean with only a slight bit of custard attached. Remove immediately from heat; custards continue to cook if stored by heat.

Neapolitan Easter Pie with Rice gluten free

I grew up eating Easter Pie, we called it Pastiera Napoletana. Many families may be more familiar with a version of this using spelt wheat grain (farro) instead of rice, resulting in the common name "Grain Pie." This is a wonderful desert to bring on visits with loved ones during the Lenten Season. Recently I discovered this amongst my maternal grandmother's recipes. I chose to make this pie with a gluten free pie crust. Delicious!

Yields 1 – 9" pie

Rice Mixture:

1 1/3 cup pre-cooked gluten free Long Grain White Rice

2/3 cup Milk

1 tablespoon Butter

½ teaspoon gluten free Vanilla Extract

In a small pot, combine milk and butter, warm milk mixture to scalding hot. Turn the heat off, add the vanilla and stir. Next, add the pre-cooked rice. Stir and fully combine. Set aside to cool completely.

Ricotta Mixture:

16 ounces creamy Ricotta

4 whole Eggs

1 Egg Yolk

¾ cup Sugar

Neapolitan Easter Pie with Rice gluten free

Pastiera Napoletana con Riso senza glutine

½ teaspoon gluten free Vanilla Extract

½ teaspoon gluten free Orange Flower Water

1 tablespoon Lemon Zest

Place the ricotta in a large bowl, add the whole eggs and the yolk.

Use a spoon to thoroughly combine the cheese and eggs. Be sure to use the back of the spoon to thin out clumps. The mixture should be as smooth as possible. Mix in the sugar, followed by the vanilla, orange flower water and lemon zest. Fold the extracts and zest into the ricotta mixture. Place aside.

Flour Mixture:

3 tablespoons gluten free Potato Starch

1 tablespoon gluten free Sorghum Flour

1/8 teaspoon gluten free Guar Gum

Combine whisk potato starch, sorghum flour and guar gum in a small bowl and place aside.

Assembling the mixtures into batter:

Pre-heat the oven to 350 degrees. Be sure the rice mixture is completely cooled. Use a fork to break up rice clumps. Add the flour mixture to the rice, use a fork to combine and coat the rice with the flour. Fold the rice into the ricotta mixture. Be sure it is thoroughly combined.

Pour the batter into the fully cooled pie shell. Place the pie shell with the batter in the center of the pre-heated oven. Bake 43-45 minutes. The center will still be tacky but solid. The top will have a golden hue. Remove from heat and completely cool. Sprinkle with confectioner's sugar and serve. Store in the refrigerator.

Pie Crust   gluten free

This pie crust has a light and flavorful dough which is ideal for sweet recipes. I make it in the food processor. I find the quick action of the plastic dough blade provides some friction and heat which helps the gluten free flours blend more succinctly.

Yields one pie crust dough

6 tablespoons gluten free Tapioca Flour

1 tablespoon gluten free Sorghum Flour

3/4 cup + 1 tablespoon gluten free Sweet Rice Flour

1 tablespoon Sugar

Pie Crust gluten free

1 teaspoon gluten free Guar Gum

½ teaspoon gluten free Baking Powder

¾ teaspoon Salt

8 tablespoons cold Butter

1 tablespoon ice Water

1 Egg, beaten

Cut cold butter into cubes ¼ - ½ inch in size. Place aside. Pour some water over ice, place aside.

Use a food processor fitted with the plastic dough blade. Measure into the bowl the tapioca, sorghum and sweet rice flours, guar gum, baking powder and sugar. Fix lid in place, pulse to combine and aerate flours.

Cut the butter into the flour in three batches, pulse often in between additions of butter. Scrape down the inside of the bowl between additions of butter.

Add the tablespoon of ice water, pulse a few times; the dough will be mostly formed very quickly. Butter the inside of an 9 inch pie baking dish. Pre-heat the oven to 350 degrees.

Remove dough from food processor. Using the palms of your hands, press dough into pie plate. Spread out from the center, use your fingers to navigate the dough up the internal edges of the baking dish. Use a fork to gently prong crust before placing it in the oven.

Beat egg, and brush a thin egg wash over the pie shell. Bake for 17-20 minutes, until just turning golden brown. Remove from oven. Cool completely before use.

Pie Crust full gluten

Traditionally prepared by hand, create a well with the flour and use a pastry blender to cut in the butter, followed by brief kneading by hand with each addition of water.

Yields one pie crust dough

1 cup All-Purpose Flour

1/3 cup cold Butter, cubed

1/8 teaspoon Salt

2-3 tablespoons Ice Water

Place flour and salt in a large bowl. Add the cubed butter in a few batches. Use a pastry blender to combine the cold butter and flour; the goal is for the dough to resemble coarse crumbs. Add the water, one tablespoon at a time.

Butter the inside of a 9 inch pie baking dish. Pre-heat the oven to 350 degrees. Knead dough a few times with hands and create a disc shape. Roll the dough out onto a floured surface. Place in buttered baking dish, trim off outer edges. Use a fork to gently prong crust before placing it in the oven.   Beat egg, and brush a thin egg wash over the pie shell.

Bake for 15-17 minutes, until just turning golden brown. Remove from oven.   Cool completely before use.

Almond Ricotta Cheesecake gluten free

A delicious crust-less cheesecake, Almond Ricotta Cheesecake uses almond meal as the flour. It is a traditional recipe, using lemon zest for an added layer of flavor. This does not always suit the American palate; I grew up with these sorts of cheesecakes and have always found them to be delicious. The traditional form of mixing would be to use a whisk and a wooden spoon in a large mixing bowl. I prefer to use a food processor with the paddle attachment.

3 cups "smooth" or "creamy" Ricotta (1 ½ pounds), room temperature

3 Whole Eggs, room temperature

1 teaspoon gluten free Vanilla Extract

½ cup + 1 tablespoon Sugar

1/3 cup Heavy Cream or Milk, room temperature

3 tablespoons Butter, melted

Lemon zest (rind of the whole lemon)

½ cup + 1 tablespoon finely ground Almond Meal

Preheat oven to 325 degrees. Butter the inside of a 9 inch pie plate. Add one tablespoon of almond meal to the plate, and rotate plate while tapping the side with your hand, to lightly cover the butter. Shake off excess.

Pour 1/3 cup of heavy cream or milk, leave aside. Grate the Lemon zest, place aside. Melt 3 tablespoons of butter, leave on warm burner on off.

Beat 3 whole eggs in small bowl, leave aside. Purchase extra smooth ricotta. Place ricotta in bowl of mixer. Mix to loosen, gradually mix eggs into ricotta.

Add lemon zest and vanilla extract, pulse to combine. Gradually process the sugar into the mixture, followed by the melted butter. Add 1/3 cup of heavy cream or milk. Mix in ½ cup almond meal, adding it in three parts, quickly pulse in between additions.

Pour into buttered pie plate. Bake 30 minutes; loosely cover with buttered foil. Then remove foil and bake an additional 10 minutes. The cheesecake will be lightly brown and springy to the touch.

Conclusion

A Note on the Passing of My Elders

The passing of my dear and beautiful Great "Uncle Gene" (Mario Eugenio Conforti) in 2011 was truly the end of an era for myself and my family. He was the last of our elders from that generation of my ancestry. He went from being my favorite Uncle to my ancestor in the blink of an eye. I had the amazing experience of growing up closely with elders from the *Old Country*, as well those from that special generation of *Italian Americans* born as in the 1920s. It is now my mother's generation who are the elders, and with them the cultural conversion of our American experiences as descendants of Italians will continue to grow and harmonize.

The last dinner I had opportunity to *"break bread"* with my Uncle Gene Conforti, was usual fare. We hugged. We ate a delicious meal prepared by my mom. We laughed. We rolled our eyes at family remarks at the table. We toasted *"Cintani!"*

Prior to our sitting at the family table, we were all gathered in my mom's kitchen. I held up Uncle Gene's bottle of Campari and signaled as if to say, "should I make you a drink?" (I held up the bottle to his attention, and pointed to a glass). He returned with a typical Italian gesture: eyes squinting, face turned slightly away, and a quick downward full hand movement – meaning "no thank you".

Then in an instant, Uncle Gene looked up and said

"No baby,

Tonight I'm going dry –

I'll just have wine with dinner."

Con tutti mi amore...

Pictured: My Great Uncles Gene Conforti and Joe Conforti respectively

✳ Endnotes:

"*Culture*" defined; Merriam Webster Dictionary; Merriam-Webster Inc.; Springfield, MA; 2004

[2] IBID

[3] UNESCO; "*About*"; http://whc.unesco.org/en/about/

[4] Wikipedia; "*Cultural Heritage*"; http://en.wikipedia.org/wiki/Cultural_heritage

[5] http://en.wikipedia.org/wiki/Gluten

[6] Fda.gov; Questions and Answers: *Gluten-Free Food Labeling Final Rule; Aug 2, 2013*;
http://www.fda.gov/Food/GuidanceRegulation/GuidanceDocumentsRegulatoryInformation/
Allergens/ucm362880.htm

[7] USC Title 21, Chapter 1, Subchapter 8, Part 101 "Food Labeling"

[8] FALCPA (Title II, of Pub L. 108-282, Section 206)

[9] Fda.gov; Questions and Answers: *Gluten-Free Food Labeling Final Rule; Aug 2, 2013*;
http://www.fda.gov/Food/GuidanceRegulation/GuidanceDocumentsRegulatoryInformation/
Allergens/ucm362880.htm

[10] USC Title 21, Chapter 1, Subchapter 8, Part 101 "Food Labeling", Section 101.91 "gluten-free"

[11] http://en.wikipedia.org/wiki/Parts_per_notation

[12] Personal email correspondence with Mccormick's; May 2013

[13] Personal email correspondence with Lawry's (McCormick) 5/10/13

[14] Personal email correspondence with Mccormick's; May 2013

[15] FALCPA (Title II, of Pub L. 108-282, Section 206)

[16] Celiac.com celiac disease and gluten free diet info since 1995 website, 5/1/13

[17] Is there Gluten in Absolut Vodka?; http://www.absolut.com/us/about/qna; September 2013

[18] Jack Daniels email correspondence to Liz Conforti dated: 5/20/2013

[19] EU Regulation EC/68/2007

[20] EFSA Opinion Summary: *Opinion of the Panel on dietetic products, nutrition and allergies
[NDA] related to a notification from CEPS on cereals used in distillates for spirits*, pursuant to
Article 6 paragraph 11 of Directive 2000/13/EC;
http://www.efsa.europa.eu/en/efsajournal/pub/484.htm ; EFSA Journal June 2007

[21] Ibid

[22] Ibid

[23] US Department of the Treasury, Alcohol & Tobacco Tax & Trade Bureau (TTB) Press Release May 22, 2012: *"TTB Issues Ruling on Gluten Labeling for Alcohol Beverages"*; http://www.ttb.gov/press/fy12/press-release12-4.pdf

[24] TTB Ruling No. 2012-2 May 24, 2012: *"Interim Policy on Gluten Content Statements in the Labeling and Advertising of Wines, Distilled Spirits, and Malt Beverages"*; http://www.ttb.gov/rulings/2012-2.pdf

[25] Gluten Free Foods & Beverages in the US , 4th Ed.; Abstract *"Packaged Facts: Insights on Consumer Markets"*; 2013; Packaged Facts is a division of Market Research LLC

[26] GFCO (Gluten Free Certification Organization) seal of authenticity on foods; gluten.net

[27] gluten.net/industry-programs-landing-page/how-to-certify,5/1/13

[28] GIG; *Producing Gluten-Free Products in a Non-Dedicated Kitchen*; April 2012; GIG; gluten.net

[29] *"Study Finds Gluten Contamination of Inherently Gluten-free Grains and Flours"*; Celiac Awareness Campaign of the US National Institutes of Health; http://celiac.nih.gov/NewsletterWinter11.aspx

[29b] Conversation with Mario Caluori January 15, 2014

[30] Conversation with Dr. Tina D'Amato, February 28, 2014

[31] Hagman, Bette; *The Gluten Free Gourmet Makes Desserts*; Henry Holt Publisher; NY; 2002

[32] American Heart Association; *Know Your Fats*; 2013; http://www.heart.org/HEARTORG/Conditions/Cholesterol/PreventionTreatmentofHighCholesterol/Know-Your-Fats_UCM_305628_Article.jsp

[33] Erasmus, Udo; *Fats that Heal/Fats that Kill*; 15th Ed.; 2004; Alive Publishing Group; BC Canada

[34] *"Chemical Leavening 101 "– Baking Powder Reaction"*; Clabber Girl Corp.; 2013

[35] *"Baking Soda"*; http://en.wikipedia.org/wiki/Baking_soda; 2013

[36] *American Heart Association Dietary Guideline 2012*; Americanheart.org

[37] Encyclopedia Britannica; *"Ice Cream"*; http://www.britannica.com/EBchecked/topic/281091/ice-cream

Bibliography:

Absolut.com; *Is there Gluten in Absolut Vodka?*;
http://www.absolut.com/us/about/qna; September 2013

American Heart Association; *American Heart Association Dietary Guideline 2012*;
heart.org;http://www.heart.org/HEARTORG/Conditions/Cholesterol/Prevent ionTreatmentofHighCholesterol/Know-Your-Fats_UCM_305628_Article.jsp

Anderson, Jane; "Gluten in Gluten Free Grains Part 1";
http://celiacdisease.about.com/b/2010/06/27/gluten-in-gluten-free-grains-part-one.htm; 2010

Anderson, Jane; "Is Soy Gluten Free?";
http://celiacdisease.about.com/od/Gluten-Free-Grains/f/Is-Soy-Gluten-Free.htm; 2012

Busycooks.com

Celiac.com; *"Celiac Disease Research Projects, Fundraising, Epidemiology, Etc."*;
http://www.celiac.com/categories/Miscellaneous-Information-on-Celiac-Disease/Celiac-Disease-Research-Projects%2C-Fundraising%2C-Epidemiology%2C-Etc./

Clabber Girl; *"Chemical Leavening 101 – Baking Powder Reaction"*; Clabber Girl Corp.; 2013;
http://www.clabbergirl.com/consumer/baking_fun/lesson_plans/chemical_101.php

Damato Dr., Tina; conversation with author; February 28, 2014

Erasmus, Udo; *Fats That Heal, Fats that Kill*; Alive Press; Canada; 1995

Erdmann Ph.D., Robert & Jones, Meirion; *Fats That Can Save Your Life*; Bio-Science Press; WA; 1998

EFSA Opinion Summary: *Opinion of the Panel on dietetic products, nutrition and allergies [NDA] related to a notification from CEPS on cereals used in distillates for spirits, pursuant to Article 6 paragraph 11 of Directive*

2000/13/EC; http://www.efsa.europa.eu/en/efsajournal/pub/484.htm; EFSA Journal June 2007

Encyclopedia Britannica; *"Ice Cream"*; http://www.britannica.com/EBchecked/topic/281091/ice-cream

European Food Safety Authority; September 2013 *"About;"* http://www.efsa.europa.eu/en/aboutefsa.htm

EU Health & Consumers Food Webpage September 2013 *"Labeling Nutrition"*: http://ec.europa.eu/food/food/labellingnutrition/nutritionlabel/index_en.htm

EU Commission Regulation (EC) No. 68/2007; *Commission Regulation of 25 January 2007 determining the extent to which applications lodged in January 2007 for import licenses..."*

EU Commission Regulation (EC) No. 178/2002; *"Defines traceability as the ability to trace and follow food, feed, and ingredients through all stages of production, processing and distribution."*

Food Allergen Labeling and Consumer Protection Act of 2004 (FALCPA), (Public Law 108-282, Title II, Section 206)

Fda.gov ; *"Questions and Answers: Gluten-Free Food Labeling Final Rule"*; http://www.fda.gov/Food/GuidanceRegulation/GuidanceDocumentsRegulatoryInformation/Allergens/ucm362880.htm; Aug 2, 2013

Fda.gov; http://www.fda.gov/Food/GuidanceRegulation/GuidanceDocumentsRegulatoryInformation/Allergens/ucm362880.htm

GFCO (Gluten Free Certification Organization)*"Seal of Authenticity on Foods";* https://www.gluten.net/industry-programs-landing-page/how-to-certify,5/1/13

GIG (Gluten Intolerance Group) certifying organization for GFCO; *Producing Gluten-Free Products in a Non-Dedicated Kitchen*; April 2012; http://www.gluten.net/wp-content/pdf/gf-in-nondedicated-kit-04-2012.pdf

Gluten Intolerance Group; Gluten.net

Hagman, Bette; The Gluten Free Gourmet Makes Dessert; Henry Holt & Co.; NY; 2002

Hagman, Bette; The Gluten Free Gourmet Bakes Bread; Henry Holt & Co.; NY; 1999

Hazen, Theodore; The Automation of Flour Milling in America, Pt.1 & Pt.2; 1996; http://www.angelfire.com/journal/millrestoration/more.html

Jack Daniels email Correspondence with author dated: 5/20/2013

Lawry's email correspondence with author dated: 5/10/13

Levy-Birnbaum, Rose; *The Cake Bible*; William Morrow & Co.; NY; 1990

McCormick email correspondence with author dated: 5/6/13, 5/9/13 and 5/10/13

Merriam Webster Dictionary

Packaged Facts, division of Market Research LLC; Gluten Free Foods & Beverages in the US , 4th Ed.; Abstract *"Packaged Facts: Insights on Consumer Markets"*; 2013

Phillips, Sarah; Baking 911.com

practicallyedible.com

scienceofcooking.com

TTB Ruling No. 2012-2 May 24, 2012: *"Interim Policy on Gluten Content Statements in the Labeling and Advertising of Wines, Distilled Spirits, and Malt Beverages"*; http://www.ttb.gov/rulings/2012-2.pdf

US Department of the Treasury, Alcohol & Tobacco Tax & Trade Bureau (TTB) Press Release May 22, 2012: *"TTB Issues Ruling on Gluten Labeling for Alcohol Beverages"*; http://www.ttb.gov/press/fy12/press-release12-4.pdf

UNESCO World Heritage Sites, Naples, Italy; http://whc.unesco.org/en/list/726

USC Title 21 "Food and Drugs"

USC Title 21, Chapter 1, Subchapter 8, Part 101*"Food Labeling"*

USC Title 21, Chapter 1, Subchapter 8, Part 101, Section 101.91 *"gluten-free"*

US Department of the Treasury, Alcohol & Tobacco Tax & Trade Bureau (TTB) Press Release May 22, 2012: "TTB Issues Ruling on Gluten Labeling for Alcohol Beverages"; http://www.ttb.gov/press/fy12/press-release12-4.pdf

US National Institutes of Health; *The Celiac Awareness Campaign of the US National Institutes of Health in "Study Finds Gluten Contamination of Inherently Gluten-free Grains and Flours"* http://celiac.nih.gov/NewsletterWinter11.aspx

Watson, F., Stone, M., & Bunning, M.; *Gluten-Free Baking*; Revised 4/09; http://www.ext.colostate.edu/pubs/foodnut/09376.html

✳ **Index:**

Made in the USA
Middletown, DE
21 December 2021

56815999R00124